SPARKLE

The Girl's Guide to Living a
DELICIOUSLY DAZZLING, WILDLY EFFERVESCENT,
KICK-ASS *Life*

CARA ALWILL LEYBA

SPARKLE

Cover art © Cara Loper/Loose Lid Creative
www.looselidcreative.com

Interior design by Ryan Leyba

Interior illustration © SANDY M

ISBN-13: 978-0-615-67580-0

Mom, this book is for you.
There are no words.
Thank you for everything.

"There comes a time in every woman's life when the only thing that helps is *a glass of champagne*."

– BETTE DAVIS

© SANDY M

CONTENTS

APERITIF
What's Champagne Got to Do with It? 1

Indulge YOUR MIND

What Makes You Sparkle? 9
Uncork Your Best Self 19
Be Here Now 27
Jealousy Will Get You Nowhere 39

Indulge YOUR BODY

Healthy is the New Skinny 49
Let's Get Physical 59
Self-Indulgence Can Save Your Life 67
When in Doubt, Be Glamorous 75

Indulge YOUR SOUL

The Happiness Cocktail 85
Matters of the Heart 91
Got to Be Real 97
The Power of Fabulous Thinking 105
Be Fearless 111

DIGESTIF
A Toast to You! 119

APERITIF
WHAT'S *Champagne* GOT TO DO WITH IT?

Think about the last time you had a beer. How did it make you feel? Aside from slightly buzzed, you probably felt bloated, tired, and a little bit like you should be riding in a pick-up truck with fingers covered in wing sauce. Now, think about the last time you had a glass of champagne. Tell me you did not feel like you should be lounging on a tufted pink chaise, wearing a pair of silk, leopard print pajamas with pearls strung around your neck (possibly even speaking with a fake French accent…).

There is something so undoubtedly sexy and glamorous about champagne. It represents luxury, elegance and the good life. Pop a bottle of champagne in your home when you have guests and you immediately command the room. People stop and turn their attention to you. You become an instant *rock star*.

I can't recall the first time I ever tasted champagne, but I can recall when I started regularly incorporating it in my life. I'll be blunt here – I did not grow up in a classic six on the Upper East Side. The closest thing we had to a housekeeper was my grandmother, and like most, I thought champagne was something reserved for the rich and famous.

So when my friend suggested I start drinking champagne while embarking on yet another one of my dieting endeavors, I laughed. *Yeah, okay*, I thought. I couldn't imagine ordering a glass of bubbly from the plump, red-nosed Irish bartender at the Midtown dive my friends and I went to after work. He'd laugh in my face and pour me a Coors Light draft.

I was never a skinny kid. Growing up in an Italian-American family meant lots of food – delicious food. Hence, the reason I have a fat ass. Always have, always will. Now, don't get me wrong, I'm not talking the kind of fat ass that takes up three plane seats.

More like the fat ass Kim Kardashian would have if she had an obsession with toasted bagels with cream cheese and gave up her 6 am workouts with Gunnar.

Food was the glue that held our family together, and the answer to all of life's problems. Fight with your boyfriend? Have a little lasagna, you'll feel better. Failed a test at school? Chicken cutlets will help. Got that promotion at work? It's time for some red wine and pasta! Food was there when you were happy, and when you were sad. It was therapy. Most often in the form of a crusty loaf of Italian bread slathered in Breakstone's butter, or in a heaping plate of gooey, cheesy eggplant parmigiana (are you salivating yet?). In my eyes, mozzarella was one of the basic food groups and things like whole wheat bread and apples just weren't part of the equation.

Hello? It's no wonder all of those wonderfully cheesy meals did a number to my body. Year after year, I grew chubbier and chubbier and by fifth grade I had joined Weight Watchers for the first time. Being weighed in front of a room full of people at the age of eleven does not exactly do wonders for your self-esteem. But I needed some discipline and in the short-term, I did lose some weight. But a few months later I gained it back, and went on to repeat this cycle for nearly twenty years.

Through those years of yo-yo dieting, I tried every fad diet under the sun. From Jenny Craig and Weight Watchers to Atkins and South Beach, everyone got a piece of the fat-free pie. My life was a flurry of frozen diet dinners and low-calorie cookies. The women who ran the front desks of the local weight loss centers (you know, the ones who wear the Christmas sweaters and eat candy to taunt you while you weigh in like cattle?) knew me on a first-name basis. Nothing worked, and I always wound up feeling worse than when I started.

To top it all off, the lack of confidence due to my weight issues led me down a road of not only unhealthy food choices, but unhealthy relationships as well. I was so down on myself that I didn't believe I deserved a man who treated me with respect. I mean, who was gonna love the chubby chick? So I spent the bulk of my twenties surrounding myself with men who made me feel like I wasn't worthy of real, unconditional love.

In addition to the toxic relationships, I felt empty inside. I was not pursuing the things that made me happy. I had no hobbies, I wasn't working out, and I was barely even going out with friends anymore. I was lacking passion in my life in a major way. I threw myself into working long hours at a mind-numbing job, leaving no room for the things that truly lit me up. I was lost physically, emotionally and spiritually. It wasn't cute.

It was not until a good friend and coworker at MTV approached me one afternoon as I was (loudly) venting my dieting woes to another group of coworkers. Sensing my frustration, Liron decided to give me some unsolicited advice that would change my world forever. It didn't matter what I wanted to hear, this loud-mouthed firecracker was going to impart her wisdom, and it was going to be the best thing that had ever happened to me.

Liron assured me that if I trashed the idea of traditional dieting and started to eat for the sake of my health, I'd be home free. Recommending a meal regimen awash with fresh fruits, vegetables, whole grains and lean protein, I'd have more energy and feel better than ever. The weight, she promised, would come off in time, but most importantly I'd be healthy. Health? What was that? I was such a stranger to feeling good that I never even considered eating for the sake of my well-being.

And the best part was, Liron promised I wouldn't have to sacrifice the things I love to get there. Working like a madwoman deserves some sort of reward in my book. Some people like a piece of cake as a treat after a long day, I prefer to suck down a cocktail or two, or three. Liron suggested I trade in beer and sugary mixed drinks and enjoy a glass or two champagne because of the fact that it's only 100 calories per glass. Couple that with the fact that I felt like Zsa Zsa Gabor while drinking it and I was *sold*.

Along with my newfound passion for all things sparkling, I also developed a nightly ritual. Whenever I enjoyed my bubbles, I made sure to toast to something that day – anything. Whether it was nailing a presentation at work, or patting myself on the back for fighting through that workout, or simply getting through the day without committing homicide, there was something worth toasting. Some people pray. Some people meditate. I toast. It's my own little ritual and it works. And here's another tip girls: you don't have to drink champagne every night to take part in your evening toasts. Sparkling water spiked with delicious fresh fruit works perfectly. Just use your prettiest glass and clink away.

My sparkling transformation was doing wonders for my self-esteem. I never felt sexier and I never felt healthier. I was developing an undeniable confidence while accepting my body: curves, lumps, bumps and all. Sure, I lost a few pounds, but I also came to realize that I would never be a size two and that was totally fine. Suddenly it wasn't about getting skinny anymore. It was about feeling my best. I felt unstoppable. Gone were the days of sugar-laden cocktails and caloric beers. I was trading in greasy French fries and hot dogs for beautiful greens. I started eating fruit at night instead of "diet" ice cream as my snack. I carried myself better. I began to view champagne as a metaphor for my new life. Whenever I enjoyed a glass of champagne, I felt beautiful, sexy and worthy.

I also put an end to the toxic relationships that plagued my love life. There was no time for men who did not love me as much as I loved myself. I was no longer spending energy on relationships that did not make feel happy, loved, and satisfied.

Feeling revived and rejuvenated, I set out to ignite my passion. I had always loved writing, but never had the confidence to pursue it as a part of my life. I took the leap and started a blog to document my experiences called "The Champagne Diet" (now, "The Champagne Diaries"). The name is a metaphor, which reflects the way I decided to start living my life: effervescently. I noticed that when I drank champagne, I felt beautiful, luxurious and glamorous. I was a "Champagne Girl" now, and I was indulging in a new way of living that was all about celebrating myself – flaws included. My new sparkling outlook was contagious, and soon I was inspiring other women to celebrate themselves as well. Within three short years, my blog had been featured in *Glamour, Shape, Cosmopolitan* South Africa, *The Daily Mail* UK, *Café Mom*, and a host of other magazines and newspapers around the globe. I was passionate about sharing my message and connecting with women all around the world who were Champagne Girls, too.

Let me be clear here. This isn't all just about drinking bubbly. In fact, you don't have to drink champagne at all in order to indulge in a champagne makeover. Lord knows I don't drink every night. But I am going to use champagne as our metaphor throughout this book. Like I mentioned earlier, we reserve champagne for celebrations, but shouldn't we be celebrating every day? Shouldn't we strive to celebrate every single thing about ourselves – flaws and all?

All of these things led me to want to learn more about wellness. I was so passionate about my own lifestyle overhaul that I wanted to be able to help other women turn their own lives around. I became a certified professional life and wellness coach and have learned so much about the relationships we have with ourselves and our bodies. I now work with women one-on-one and help them pursue their passions, live healthy, delicious lives, and truly embrace who they are. Someone once described life coaching to me as taking someone from "functional to optimal." Well, I'm going to help take you from functional to *fabulous*.

My inspiration for writing this book is simple. I want every woman know she is amazing. I want her to stop obsessing over her weight and start feeling like sex on a stick no matter what size jeans she wears. I want her to feel like she is worthy of a glorious, sparkling glass of champagne the way she is worthy of a healthy and happy relationship. I want her to toast to herself each night and learn to appreciate all the good things about her life.

So, I welcome you on this journey with me. You are about to embark on a complete lifestyle overhaul. You are about to feel like the glamorous goddess you know you are. You're going to radically redefine happiness and start living life on your own terms. You're going to learn to rejuvenate your senses with luxurious rituals that help you clear the clutter in your mind and feel energized. You're going to discover what makes you come alive. So go grab a glass and get ready to sparkle Champagne Girls, *it's on.*

Indulge YOUR MIND

CHAPTER 1
WHAT MAKES YOU *Sparkle*?

"Don't ask what the world needs. Ask what makes
you come alive, and go do it. Because what the
world needs is people who have come alive."
– *Howard Thurman*

In a perfect world, it's 2 am and I'm spinning on a dance floor
in Chelsea to George Michael's "Freedom." I'm surrounded by a
gaggle of gay men and I'm on my fourth Cosmo without a care
in the world. My only concern is that I need to wake up the next
day by noon to get ready for my appearance on *The Today Show*.
And I have a pedicure appointment.

Insert "needle on the record" sound effect.

In reality, it's 2 am and I'm tossing and turning in bed, wondering if I remembered to send that last email before leaving
work. I'm trying to recall whether or not I have meetings the
next day and if so, what I'll wear so I can appear semi-profes-
sional, but not look like K.D. Lang. Shit, do I need to iron anything? And most importantly – do we have coffee in the house?

The delicate balance between making a living and living a passionately creative life is something that pains many of us daily. It's
a harsh reality when you realize you weren't left a trust fund, and
that Carrie Bradshaw's rent stabilized apartment on the Upper
West Side doesn't really exist (at least not for $750 a month). Life
can be brutal – especially when you need to make money.

As fabulous as it would be to live out our dreams twenty-four
hours a day, most of us just can't. There are things that need to get
done. Some of us have to keep a day job, at least temporarily, to
pay bills until we can pursue those dreams. We have responsibili-

ties that can distract us from doing the things that we love to do. But that doesn't mean we can't maximize our downtime to pursue all of those dreams that often get the back seat – but I'll get to that in a minute. You may be reading this and thinking: *I don't have anything that I'm passionate about.* And that, my darlings, is what we need to fix immediately.

To truly sparkle, you need to figure out what it is that turns you on. Now here's where I put on my Life Coach Tiara. I want you to ask yourself: what really gets your mental engine revved up? Besides a salty plate of French fries and a giant goblet of pinot noir (oh, wait… maybe that's just me?). What is the one thing that gets you out of bed in the morning and gets you going? What gets you off your ass? What makes you come alive?

I'm not trying to get all deep here and tell you that you should be out on the street rescuing kittens for a living or sending $27 a month to an infomercial to keep endangered birds alive. I'm not even telling you that you need a career overhaul in order to be passionate about your life. But, if you search within yourself, I am sure there is something that ignites the flames in your little brain and gives you that fuzzy feeling inside. Because when our champagne buzz wears off, we need something that can still make us feel all tingly.

Passionate people are the ones who
keep us watching them.

The most interesting people in this world are passionate. They radiate inspiration. We want to be around them. We are drawn to them, and we often look to them for motivation. Whether they are entrepreneurs, actors, writers, doctors, mothers, or pet clothing designers, they all share something in common and that is the fact that they love what they do. Passionate people are the ones who keep us watching them.

The passions in my own life have changed from time to time, and that's what makes things interesting. If you had asked me at seventeen years old what I wanted to do with my career, I would have told you that I wanted to be a music journalist. Music was – and still is – my life. Throughout my teen years, I lived and breathed *Spin* and *Rolling Stone*. I was obsessed with MTV News. I idolized Tabitha Soren. I spent four out of seven nights a week at concerts, and it wasn't because I wanted to stare at the hot musicians, although that *was* a nice perk.

Seeing the rhinestone lining in every situation
will allow you to work past the disappointment of
losing something, and instead, pull yourself up by
the stilettos and work toward being better
the next time around.

As the years went on, I realized it wasn't so easy to get a full-time job at a music magazine. Even countless hours spent interning at the biggest music companies in the world still didn't guarantee me full-time work. But I never gave up. Even when I got fired from a prominent record label at twenty-three for affectionately referring to one of my bosses as "Chuck Goldenfuck" over an IM conversation with my best friend.

In retrospect, getting fired was probably one of the best things that ever happened to me, because it allowed me to a) realize that in corporate America, and in life, and you need to be buttoned up at all times and b) it has provided my friends and I with endless hours of belly laughs for the past ten-plus years. I was always good at nick names, and I'm pretty sure that one will go down in history. Seeing the rhinestone lining in every situation will allow you to work past the disappointment of losing something, and instead, pull yourself up by the stilettos and work toward being better the next time around.

My career took a left turn and by the time I was twenty-six, I wound up working for MTV in their digital advertising department. I hadn't exactly envisioned myself working on Oreo campaigns and analyzing website traffic for a living, but I was working for MTV, and I was passionate about the brand. I may not have shared a cubicle with Kurt Loder, but I knew I could network my way through that building and eventually live out my wild seventeen-year-old journalistic fantasies.

With a lot of hard work, perseverance, and thick skin, I finally got in touch with the right people and before I knew it, I was pitching stories and getting them published on MTV.com. But it wasn't all roses. I didn't get paid for my stories because I worked full-time for the company. I got rejected constantly. I still had to do my day job. And I was exhausted.

But none of that mattered because I was passionate about what I was doing. I'd set my alarm an hour early each morning, sift through all the entertainment news on my little broken down pink laptop, and pitch story after story before I got in the shower. By the time 9 am rolled around, I'd have replies from my editor. I'd work my regular job through the morning, and when lunch time rolled around I'd eat at my desk and work on edits. By 6 pm, I'd frantically scour the site and search for my published pieces. Each time one went up, it felt like the first time. I was ecstatic to see all my hard work come to fruition.

By that summer, I had proved myself to be hungry and relentless when it came to getting stories. I never gave up, even when I got rejected. My editor called me one evening, just as I was about to leave for the day, and asked if I was interested in covering the MTV Video Music Awards. *Was I interested?* This had been my dream since high school. Every year I'd watch the show and tell my mother, "One day I will be there." My heart nearly beat out of my chest as I agreed to take on the job. I covered the award show as an "embedded reporter" and had a front row seat. I remember walking up to Radio City Music Hall, taking a deep breath, and feeling like I had truly arrived. I soaked in every moment that night: the hot, bright lights, the roar of the crowd, and the fact that I had finally gotten to the place that I had always wanted to be. I wrote my article at 2 am that morning, and by the next day it had garnered millions of readers. This is without a doubt still one of my proudest achievements and a night I will never, ever forget.

My passion now is connecting with and inspiring women. It's helping them reinvent themselves and make their lives worth living. It's encouraging them to kick all the bullshit out of their lives and start focusing on the great. My passion is helping other women become passionate.

So here we go. You are now on a mission to ignite the flames of your soul. That sounds so intense, doesn't it? But I'm not sending you off to the fire alone. I'm going to hold your hand the whole way through. You will not get burned if you follow these rules of the road. They are the things you need to keep in mind. Your mantras. Now let's begin.

Your Passion Will Turn You On

You know that flip-floppy feeling you get in your stomach when you're on a really great date? Or when you first kiss that hot guy you are completely obsessed with? Well, that's the feeling you should get when you are doing what you love to do. And this is even better, because your passion can't break up with you, cheat on you, be bad in bed, or fight with you, so that fabulous feeling is here to stay.

When you have realized your dream, it will consume your senses. It may keep you awake at night, or it may catapult you from bed in the morning. It will have a physical effect on you, somehow. It'll make your heart race, your blood pump, give you goose bumps, and make your head spin. It'll be riveting and exciting, and it will give you an overwhelming sense of joy. In other words, *it will turn you the hell on.*

Finding your passion isn't always a simple task. It takes some digging to figure out what really excites you. Start by asking yourself some questions that may seem obvious, but may be a sign of what's brewing in your brain. If money weren't an issue, what would your dream job be? If you could live anywhere in the world, and do anything, what would it be? What do you find yourself doing most in your spare time?

Try to focus on what excites you. I personally have a laundry list of mini obsessions. For one, I totally admire women's romance writers. My secret dream job would be to run away to London and write novels about hot-blooded affairs and steamy, muscular men named Lucas. Who ride horses. Weird? Maybe. But it's a fun little fantasy that gets me riled up. I find that I'm always googling these authors, researching what their lives are like, obsessively reading their Twitter feeds and Facebook pages, watching their YouTube videos. And who knows? Maybe one day I'll turn that fantasy into a reality.

So what gets you going? What do you always find yourself reading about? What jobs are you envious of? Hone in on your day dreams, there may be more to them than you think.

Your Passion Will Empower You

Once you've discovered what it is that turns you on, you'll probably realize that you feel in control when you're doing it.

Even if you're not fully confident in your newfound passion, you'll feel happy that you're actually taking steps toward your goal, and in turn that will empower you. Your passion will give you strength. You will feel unstoppable.

Of course, you're human, so there will be moments when you doubt yourself and wonder what the hell you're doing, but at the core, you will feel energized, vibrant and luminous. And you will feel equipped to deal with whatever comes your way. Even when I found myself in the middle of the MTV Video Music Awards, with no idea what I was doing or what to expect, I still made it work. I was thrilled to be there, and my passion is what got me through. When you love what you do, there is always a way to make it happen. And you, my delicious Goddess, will always figure out how.

Having a Passion Will Keep You Healthy

But it's not all just about getting your rocks off. Having a passion in life, which leads to a sense of purpose, will also keep you sane – literally. A recent study from the Rush Alzheimer's Disease Center shows that having a purpose in life will actually protect your brain against disease. People with a clear purpose in life have slower rates of mental decline, the research shows, even as plaques and tangles developed in their brains. Those plaques and tangles that form in our brains as we age affect memory and have been linked with Alzheimer's disease.

Finding something you are passionate about will also ward off depression. Think about how sad and lonely it is to feel like a drone doing the same thing day in and day out. Sitting at the same cubicle all day long is a slow suicide. Feeling like its Groundhog's Day every day does absolutely nothing for your creative juices. But when you have something to focus on that's new and challenging (even if it's after-hours or on weekends), you start exercising different muscles of the brain and you begin to come alive.

This Ain't Your Mama's Dream

In addition to feeling empowered, in control (and avoiding going insane in the membrane), you have to keep in mind that your passion should be your own. This ain't your mama's dream. Champagne Girls are authentic creatures. Whatever you are passionate about must come from a place of sincerity. It has to be *your* thing. Not what you think your parents want you to do. Not what you think will get you ahead somehow. It's got to be truly, genuinely, wholeheartedly you.

So many of us are chasing goals that are not our own. We're in med school because that's what our parents always told us we should do. We're running the family business because we feel like we should. We're studying to be lawyers because our father was a lawyer, and his father was a lawyer, and so on. If you are living someone else's dream, you are wasting your life – plain and simple. It's time to take your passion and put it in the front seat. Your life is meant to be lived by you, and for you. Your parents will get over it.

Blaze your own glittery, sparkly, fiery, shimmering path. Surround yourself with the things that make you shine. Create your bubble and thrive in it.

None of this is easy. Finding your passion takes time, and effort, but it's worth every second. To truly sparkle, you'll need to do some serious soul-searching. You're going to have to put some elbow grease into this. In the words of RuPal, "*You. Betta. Work.*" And I don't want to hear any whining! Self-discovery is the biggest gift you can give yourself. So get into it. Blaze your own glittery, sparkly, fiery, shimmering path. Surround yourself with the things that make you shine. Create your bubble and thrive in it. Don't wait another second. At the risk of sounding cliché, we've only got one life to live, so let's live it passionately.

CHAPTER 2
Uncork YOUR BEST SELF

"Accept everything about yourself – I mean everything, You are you and that is the beginning and the
end – no apologies, no regrets."
– *Clark Moustakas*

Chasing our passions and figuring out what makes us sparkle
is crucial, but we can't get there if we aren't confident. And as
women, we have mastered the art of being professionally criti-
cal of ourselves. From crash diets and plastic surgery to wrinkle
creams and colonics, we've done it all and then some. We've read
books on why men like bitches, and strived to be more of a bitch.
We've read articles on why we should stop eating bread to lose
weight, and we've stopped eating bread (and, God, *wasn't that
hard?*) We're constantly being told that we should look younger,
be skinnier, have fuller lips, act a certain way to obtain the job we
think we should have, and we've bought into it all. And frankly,
I am over it.

It's time to start celebrating ourselves! We've come a long
way, baby. Women are now mothers, wives, girlfriends, profes-
sionals, executives, students, politicians, doctors, teachers – the
list goes on. We're beautiful, we're strong and we are empowered,
and we have carved a pretty unique niche into this world. We've
proved that we can do it all. Raise the children, run the house-
hold, and run the boardroom – sometimes all in the same day. In
short, we're pretty damn amazing.

So let's stop obsessing over our flaws and start toasting to
the deliciously authentic creatures we are. Let's get our attitudes
in check and start appreciating all the fabulous things we are

blessed with. Let's rock our best *ass*-ets and forget about the rest. Sound good? Good. But first, we'll need to change our mindset.

In order to begin to uncork your best self, you need to believe in the good and ignore the bad. Because someone will *always* have something to say.

One of the most frustrating things we do as women is hear only the negative. Six people can tell us we look beautiful on a particular day, but we'll still hear that demonic whisper of our ex-boyfriend that told us that we needed to lose weight. We don't hear the six compliments we got that morning; instead we are hell-bent on that prick that told us we were fat. Five years ago. Well, it's time to kick all that crap to the curb. Take out the emotional trash, so to speak. In order to begin to uncork your best self, you need to believe in the good and ignore the bad. Because someone will *always* have something to say.

Taking out the Trash

We all have "energy vampires" in our lives. Those people who always seem to know how to zap the fun right out of us. The ones who call our phones relentlessly, until we pick up, and only talk about themselves. Unless you're a cold-hearted snake, you probably let these people steamroll you from time to time with their mindless drama. I am guilty as charged, but I've put an end to it. I've given myself a "get out of jail free" card and realized that I cannot – and should not – try to save the world. It's draining, and it takes away from time that you could be focusing on yourself (a much more exciting project).

And then there are the criticizers. The people in your life, be it friends, or family, even lovers, who love to pass judgment on everything you do. The ones whose phone calls you can't ignore, and when you pick up, they are ready to jump down your throat about anything and everything. Maybe it's the shade of lipstick you're wearing, or the new haircut you just got, or the career choice you've made – whatever it is, these people have a way to rain all over your parade. And they can have a serious effect on our confidence.

So how do we ignore the negativity and let that bubbly lady out to play, regardless of the naysayers? It might seem like one of life's most impossible tasks when you're "in it." When you're in that toxic relationship – whether it be with a man, or a family member, or even a friend – who constantly tries to bring you down, it's hard to see past the ridicule. Well, I'll state the obvious here: the first step is to *get the hell away*. Honestly, run. Easier said than done, believe me, but it's a must. The longer you keep those people in your world, the longer you will remain controlled by their wrath. A good rule of thumb is: if someone is around who brings you down, it's time to take out the trash. And if you can't eliminate them completely, then seriously reevaluate how much time you give them. Life is way too short for drama and negativity.

Reality Check

The second step is recognizing all of the fabulous things about yourself that you held hostage while you were surrounded by the nasty little voices (aka your annoying, judgmental childhood friend or rude ex-boyfriend). It might take some time to learn to be yourself again, but let me tell you, when the flood gates open, the world better watch out. You're going to feel more empowered than ever. Those voices that held you back will be silenced forever.

So here's our first exercise. As a rule of thumb, I want you to feel totally free to have a glass of wine or champagne when you complete each one. Why? Because it's more fun that way. If you don't drink, a glass of sparkling water in a beautiful champagne flute will do (it's all about the glamour!) But be careful ladies, only one glass. That's about five ounces. And I'm counting! You don't want to wind up drunk-dialing when you should be on the road to self-discovery because *that* ain't cute.

So grab a pen and paper, and get ready to make a list. In your "pros" column, you're going to list out all of the ways you feel when you've eliminated this toxic person from your life and "taken out the trash." If you haven't given them the boot yet, list out the way you feel when they're not around. Some words that may come to mind: relieved, liberated, happy, peaceful, beautiful, confident and sane. And sanity is *very* important. In the "cons" column, I want you to list all of the ways you feel when this person is in your life. Some words you may choose to list: neurotic, paranoid, smothered, judged, overwhelmed, unloved, and unworthy. It should become pretty clear that you are much happier without this person around. And who can blame you?

Now, take a look at that "pros" list again. Those very feelings and qualities are the things that are innately within you: the raw, uninhibited, beautiful qualities that make you authentically you. And that Hefty Cinch Sak of emotional shit is prohibiting you from being all of those things. Don't you just want to go punch something? Go ahead, I'll wait.

Now that you've uncorked the qualities that make you so wonderful, and eliminated the bullshit from your life, you are officially on the road liberation and authenticity. But there are a few more things you'll need to do before you can pop the champagne and start celebrating the fabulous new you.

The Gratitude Attitude

As a life coach, one of the exercises I have my clients do is make a list of all the things they are grateful for. I advise doing this twice a day: first in the morning as a way to jump start your day, and again at night before bed. Reminding yourself of all the things you're thankful for is a great habit to form.

When you rock a "gratitude attitude," you take nothing for granted and it's a hell of a lot easier to deal with a bad day when you are conscious of the fact that it's really never that bad. It's so easy to get caught up in a temper tantrum when we miss our bus on the way to work, or get drenched in the rain, but if you really think about it, we're lucky to have those problems. Things can always be worse.

Drinking champagne is an experience,
and toasting to something in your life that you
are grateful for is a fun way to tie in a
healthy habit to that experience.

And studies show that people who keep gratitude journals are more successful in accomplishing personal goals. Researchers from the University of California, Davis, selected a group of people and asked them to record five things each week that they were grateful for. The study reported that after two months, those people not only excelled in their goals that they had set for themselves; they also exercised more and felt better physically. Talk about a win/win situation!

And wait – it gets better. That same study showed that people who kept gratitude journals also slept better and were well-rested. So the next time you find yourself tossing and turning, start thinking about all the things you're thankful for and you may drift off to dream land sooner than expected.

So let's give this gratitude thing a whirl. If you're still drinking your bubbles from the last exercise, raise that glass and toast to one thing you are thankful for. I love gratitude toasts. In fact, it's something I do every time I drink champagne and I always make my girlfriends do it with me. Drinking champagne is an experience, and toasting to something in your life that you are grateful for is a fun way to tie in a healthy habit to that experience.

If you're out of champagne, then get your pen and paper. Start a list of whatever you appreciate in your life – big or small. Things you can include are your job, your friendships, your family, your pet, your health, or the fact that you have a really great ass – whatever. Get creative. No item is too silly.

Shake What Your Mama Gave Ya

If I could identify one glaring quality that all fabulous women possess it would be this: they know their best ass-et and they rock it like the rent is due tomorrow. Living effervescently is not about obsessing over what's wrong; it's about accentuating what's right. It's about finding what works and playing it up.

Maybe you're not where you want to be weight-wise (who is?) But who gives a shit? Stop waiting to lose ten pounds to buy new clothes. Buy them now. Find flattering clothes and dress for the body you have now – not the body you want next summer. Do the things that make you feel glamorous and sexy. The more you avoid them, the worse you will feel.

And as for the rest – work with what you've got. Have big thighs? Buy more dresses that hug those curves. Got a muffin top lingering? Buy a blousy peasant top and put it with a pair of a kick-ass black pants. Make it work, girl! Treat yourself to things that make you feel good and look good.

And most importantly, stop being so damn hard on yourself. Perfection is a myth. Once you give up the notion that you have to reach an impossible goal to feel good, you'll be surprised at how easy it all becomes.

CHAPTER 3
BE HERE *Now*

"Breathe. Let go. And remind yourself
that this very moment is the only one you
know you have for sure."
– *Oprah Winfrey*

When I was twenty-two, I wore a size eight. For about five minutes. During those five minutes, I high-tailed it to Bloomingdales and spent close to $200 on a pair of designer jeans. God, how I loved those jeans! They were faux-faded denim, with intricate stitching on the back pockets and purposeful holes in the knees. They screamed "I'm not really poor, I'm just fashionable," and I rocked the shit out of them.

Because a size eight wasn't normal for me, the minute I looked at a carbohydrate I puffed right back up to a size twelve – my happy place – and I was no longer able to get those stylish little puppies past my thighs. I felt like a failure. All the skinny girls were wearing ripped up designer denim, and I was back in frump-wear. I was once again shopping for wide leg Old Navy jeans, the kind that new moms bought for that two month period after giving birth where they still sort of looked pregnant. Except I wasn't a new mom. And I had run out of excuses.

I still, however, kept the faith that one day I'd sausage my juicy ass back into those designer pants. So much so that I got them dry cleaned, and hung them neatly in my closet (in the plastic, of course) so they'd be in perfect shape for their coming out party as soon as I lost ten pounds. I assumed I'd look at them as motivation, and every time I wanted to eat fistfuls of cupcakes, I'd hop back to my closet, eye the jeans, and then wink at the camera as if I were in a Weight Watchers commercial. The Pointer Sisters "New Attitude" would play loudly, and I'd have a giant glossy smile on my face, content and totally free of my desire to gorge on sweet treats, because I was getting back into those jeans, damn it.

Fast forward one year later, and I decided to give them another whirl. I had been working out like a crazy woman (this is around the time Spin classes got popular), so I was positive I'd slide right into those bad boys. I'd scoff at the old memory of me trying to tuck my butt cheeks into them one year prior.

Yeah? Well, think again.

Sure I was eating healthy (kind of), but I was also climbing virtual mountains three times a week to the 125 bpm version of "Stayin' Alive" by The Bee Gees, so my legs got bulkier. Bulky muscle on an already curvy frame is a recipe for disaster when it comes to designer clothes. Famous designers make clothes for paper dolls, not workout-obsessed Guidettes from Brooklyn. Down but not out, I decided to keep the faith – and the jeans.

Throughout the next five years, I'd stare at the denim inspiration hanging in my closet, becoming more and more fearful to attempt putting them on again. I was getting older, and I was definitely not getting skinnier. I tried different diets and exercise routines, but I never seemed to get back to that size eight I flirted with at the tender age of twenty-two. I racked my brain to figure out how to be that thin again, and each obsessive moment became more and more detrimental to my mental well-being.

After a good seven (yes, seven) years of staring at these jeans, I found myself at a crossroads. I was cleaning out my closet one Saturday afternoon, getting ready to donate clothes to my local church, and I came face to face with my denim alter ego. All of a sudden, it hit me: I had to say goodbye. I had been hanging onto this ideal that was no longer a part of me. In fact, it never really was. I fit those jeans because I starved myself into them. They weren't me. And I had become so hung up on how I looked in them years prior, judging myself constantly because they no longer fit. There I was, pushing twenty-nine years old, defining myself by my past.

I started to accept the fact no matter how hard I tried, I might never be a size eight again. The ironic thing is I was healthier than ever. I was eating a pretty balanced diet (of course, with the occasional pig-out session), working out regularly, and making smart choices that made my life better and better. I had gotten a great promotion at work. I ended a romantic relationship that had proved to be the main cause of stress in my life. So what if I wasn't skinny? Life was good. I grabbed the jeans and tossed them in a garbage bag. And I never felt freer.

By constantly obsessing over the past – or the future – we lose sight of what is happening at this very moment. We miss out on all the good stuff.

The point of my little story? By constantly obsessing over the past – or the future – we lose sight of what is happening at this very moment. We miss out on all the good stuff. I spent so much time obsessing over getting into those damn jeans that I was missing out on my life. I was missing out on all the fabulous new jeans I could have bought. I was missing out on giant, delicious bowls of pasta I could have savored. I was missing out on enjoying my new body and all the other wonderful things happening for me. Who cared if I wasn't a size eight? Was it really even that important?

Living in the moment seems like such a simple concept, doesn't it? You don't have to do much to physically be present aside from – well, breathing. But to be present emotionally and mentally can take a great deal of discipline. Our brains are constantly racing. We barely get through one task before we are thinking about the next. I can't even remember what I ate for breakfast this morning because while I was eating breakfast, I was thinking of what I'd have for lunch, and if there would be enough time in between work and meetings to cook dinner tonight.

It's crucial to bring yourself back down to Earth on a regular basis. If you don't, you'll find yourself depressed and anxious, and that's not very effervescent now is it? If you want to give your life a champagne makeover, you are going to need to get a grip. How are you going to celebrate yourself if your brain is scrambled eggs? There are a few simple tricks to getting yourself centered that every Champagne Girl needs to know.

Breathe and Sip

One of my favorite ways to ground myself is to breathe deeply. It's seriously one of the easiest things you can do to feel centered. It's free, you can do it anywhere, and the sense of relief you get after doing it is truly remarkable. Taking a few deep breaths really does remind us to take a step back, put all of the stress and anxiety off to the side (because it *will* be there when you get back), and just feel. When is the last time you just acknowledged your feelings without reacting to them?

And deep breathing does wonders for our bodies, too. Did you know that we release 70% of our toxins by breathing? And when you're stressed out, and not breathing correctly, you start taking really shallow breaths which means your brain isn't getting the right amount of oxygen. Oxygenation of the brain releases excessive anxiety, which in turn clears the mind. See why it's so important to inhale and exhale, kittens?

I personally love to do this at night after I pour a glass of wine. (Are you shocked?) I know, I know, we're trying to get the toxins *out*, not in, but I'm talking one glass here – not a bottle – at least not all the time. Before I take my first sip, I sit up really straight and take three deep breaths. As I breathe out, I let all of the stress go. I clear the clutter out of my head and actually picture a big pink broom sweeping aside my thoughts (it has to be pink for me, you can visualize whatever color you like). By my third breath, I'm feeling rejuvenated and decompressed. Then, I take a sip of my wine. It totally turns my happy hour into a little ritual and I really look forward to it after a long, stressful day. Some people prefer to spend an hour at yoga class, or meditate in the dark. I prefer to take a few deep breaths and enjoy a cocktail. To each her own, right?

Shake it!

The next time you're all wound up and feeling like you're headed straight to the loony bin, try taking a walk, or going for a run at the gym. Not only will a quick workout boost endorphins, it'll distract you from the sometimes scary thoughts that tend to take us over when we're not paying attention. And boy, can they be scary.

A few years ago, I found myself going through a really rough time. I remember marching into my therapist's office evening and demanding he refer me out to someone who could prescribe me the highest level of anti-depressants available. I was miserable and I wanted the hardcore stuff. When he began asking me what was wrong, I explained how overwhelmed I felt. Looming feelings about finances, work, family drama and relationship issues had morphed into a cocktail of anxiety that was just too much to bear. My brain was going 900 mph and I couldn't chill out.

"Are you working out?" my doctor asked. No, I certainly was not working out; in fact, I was glued to my desk ten hours a day.

When weekends rolled around, I was so drained from stressing myself out all week at work that I remained parked on the sofa with my hand planted firmly in a bag of potato chips. "Not as much as I used to," I answered, trying to hide the fact that I wasn't really the complete sloth I had turned into. "I'm going to give you a prescription. And it's to report to the gym, immediately," he told me.

Desperate to feel semi-human again, yet skeptical of his suggestion, I headed to the gym that night. I was bored of the same old treadmill/free weight rigmarole, so I begged the girl at the front desk to pair me up with a personal trainer who would stimulate my muscles and my brain. She scheduled an appointment for me to meet with a trainer who specialized in Muay Thai boxing, and I showed up the next night, ready to punch and kick my way into happiness. Would I rather have eaten Prozac for dinner? Absolutely. It was the easy way out. But instead, I sweat my way through it, and after my first thirty-minute session I felt like I was on top of the world. A good workout and the time to focus on exactly what I was doing was just what the doctor ordered, literally. I didn't think about my job, or my boyfriend, or my friend who was having her own nervous breakdown who needed me. I just focused on moving and feeling good.

Duke University did a study that showed exercise was just as successful in treating depression as drugs. And the best part? You don't have to spend hours in a kick boxing class or even invest in a personal trainer. If your budget is tight, go for a light jog around your neighborhood. Hell – do some jumping jacks in your apartment! I've had to get creative with my workouts when I didn't have the cash for a gym membership. There are no excuses. According to the British Journal of Sports Medicine, twenty minutes per week will have a significant improvement on your mental health.So put down the pills and grab a pair of sweatpants, ladies. Sanity is closer thank you think.

For the majority of my life I truly
believed that being overwhelmed and stressed at all
times was the only way to be successful, and now
I've realized that slowing down is sometimes the
most important thing you can do.

Take a Time Out

I don't know about you, but I have always been addicted to being busy. I constantly have to be working on at least a few projects, and dreaming up new ones, all the while juggling my real life. As the self-proclaimed queen of to-do lists, I can tell you that I tend to bite off more than I can chew most days of the week. And that really is a recipe for disaster, especially if you plan on actually doing any of those tasks with a focused and clear mind. It's daunting, and I'm working on taming it.

For the majority of my life I truly believed that being overwhelmed and stressed at all times was the only way to be successful, and now I've realized that slowing down is sometimes the most important thing you can do. It wasn't until I started closely examining other women business owners that I admired (you'll read more about that in the next chapters) that I started to fully understand how important it is to be present in the moment as often as you can.

If you're anything like me, this can be a big adjustment, so try taking on one very small task at a time. It may sound completely ridiculous, but I practice this exercise while doing a mundane chore like laundry (something I truly detest, by the way). Laundry kicks my over-active brain into high gear. Most of the time while I'm loading the washers, I'm concocting some crazy idea for another book, developing a new business plan, figuring out what the hell I'm going to wear the next day, picturing various people naked, and wondering if we have dog food in the house. I'm probably even thinking of more things but I don't want to freak you out.

When I find myself going off the ADD deep end, I rein it in. I try to pay attention to exactly what I'm doing at that second. Maybe I'm noticing how pretty the fabric is on my favorite top, or taking note of the self-tanner stains on my robe (gross), but whatever it is, I'm focused. I'm there. And whenever I catch myself drifting off, I just put myself back in check and focus on the task at hand.

And sometimes it's more than just slowing down in the moment. Sometimes we need a serious Time Out. I'm talking days, even weeks off from whatever it is we're doing. Your body (and nasty little attitude) will probably let you know when it's time to take a breather. Whenever I'm pushing myself to the limit, I can usually tell. I'm cranky, irritable, and I'm toting a really negative outlook on things. This is usually caused by exhaustion – which you can bet you'll feel physically, too. When we're running ourselves to the ground, we're not sleeping well and we have little time to kick our feet up, so our whole system suffers.

When I was in the midst of earning my life coaching certification, my crazy meter reached new heights. I was working full-time, going to school six hours a week in the evenings, spending countless hours earning my "buddy coaching" hours, and also running my brand. I was so drained that it was getting harder and harder for me to be creative, and I felt like a total failure. I lost my ability to come up with ideas for blogs, let alone actually write them. I felt like I was zapped of my passion. Whatever little time I had left in the day, I was either sleeping, bitching, or sucking down red wine in an attempt to calm my nerves. My brain was over it.

My poor husband was the victim of my demonic behavior, and he knew it was best to steer clear of my path, because I was *not* fun to be around. I was short with my friends. I was snippy with my coworkers. The irony was that I was learning how to coach others on handling their own lives, yet mine seemed to be spiraling out of control. Another thing for me to obsess over.

I knew a self-imposed hiatus was long overdue, but I had trouble committing to it. I didn't want to miss anything. I am the kind of gal who is glued to my computer. If I'm away from Twitter, Facebook or email for more than twenty minutes, I'm convinced I'm going to miss some seriously important message that will change my life forever. What if someone really important emails me? What if I take longer than a half hour to respond to them and they lose interest or think I'm a flake? What if a fan writes something on The Champagne Diet's wall and I miss it, and don't answer, and then she thinks I'm a bitch?

The anxiety of removing myself from the things that made my heart beat scared the shit out of me, but I knew I had to do it. So, I "went dark" for about a week. I didn't blog, I recycled status updates for the fan page (which were few and far between), and I kissed Twitter goodbye. I didn't respond to emails. I took a couple of personal days off work and literally stayed in my pajamas all day and watched shitty daytime TV (I attribute this to the beginning of my obsession with Wendy Williams, by the way).

At first, I was in heaven. I finally had the peace I had longed for. For the entire first day, I thought about nothing. I entrenched myself in *The View* and *Ellen* and laughed loudly in my apartment at stupid jokes I would never have paid attention to before because I was juggling so many different things. I talked back at the TV. I ate potato chips. I boycotted showering and didn't put on a bra at all.

By Day Two, I was a little less comfortable with being "off." By this point, I was itching to check my email and the amount of tweets building up was enough to give me a brain aneurism.

I held strong and didn't cave, though it was much harder to get through an episode of *Dr. Oz* without wondering what was going on at my job.

I had to keep reminding myself that I was doing this to get better. Even though it truly sucked to feel so out of touch, it was necessary. I used various tactics to keep my brain from imploding during my staycation; the biggest savior was enjoying the great outdoors. I had been so used to sitting at a desk with my eyeballs glued to a monitor that I felt like I was physically craving fresh air. Whenever I'd start to get the twitch to log onto my computer, I'd lace up my sneakers and go for a long walk. I live right along the water, but I never make the time to actually get out there and soak up the serene setting that's literally right at my fingertips.

As soon as I felt that cool breeze sweep across my cheeks, it was like an instant sense of relief. Suddenly the need to connect wasn't so important. I started to truly take in my surroundings. I listened to the waves hit the rocks, and I took note of the way the clouds looked. I stared up into the sky and took deep breaths. I know it sounds so simple (and I totally sound like a weird hippie), but my brain was dying for this. I was falling in love with the world I knew before the internet, before the conference calls, before Twitter and before hundreds of emails a day.

By the end of my week-long break, it all started to click. I was coming up with fresh ideas, and reigniting my creative flames. And it was happening naturally. I wasn't stressed about deadlines. I was getting zapped with passion again in the shower, while cooking dinner, or walking down the street. I felt alive.

I returned back to the "other" real world more energized than ever. I was excited, rested and ready for everything. I also learned that I had to start giving myself time to tune out. I didn't have any plans to retire to Costa Rica and sell bananas for a living, but I was dedicated to making time for the simple things, at least once in a while.

So, slow down a bit ladies. Breathe. Sip. Feel. Take breaks. Take mental vacations. Take tropical vacations. Whatever you need to do to live in the moment, do it. Getting caught up in a million and one tasks and emotions is a surefire way to burn out and pretty much the opposite of a peaceful, sparkling life, wouldn't you say?

CHAPTER 4
JEALOUSY WILL GET YOU *Nowhere*

"If you're able to be yourself, then you have
no competition. All you have to do is get closer
and closer to that essence."
– *Barbara Cook*

Read this sentence until it is burned into your brain: *jealousy will get you nowhere.* In fact, spending your time being jealous of others will actually guarantee for you to fail. Know why? Because it makes you unhappy and zaps you of the energy you could be using to get shit done.

Champagne Girls sparkle on their own accord. They shine in all of their authentic glory. If you're comparing yourself to others, you're losing your own flair. You're surrendering the power of originality. Now how unsexy is that?

And it's important to remember something else, too. Never judge a book by its cover. There is always more to the story. I'll never forget a few years ago I became totally obsessed with this blog. I'll keep it nameless because I don't want to call anyone out, but in my eyes, the author of this blog had the life. She was not only gorgeous and smart, she was loaded, well-traveled, married to a hot guy, had the most insane house, and she was a great writer to boot. Hello? Everything I've ever wanted! I'd read her blog every single day, stalk her photos, and totally live vicariously through this chick. She had it made. Until I found out, she didn't.

One day she posted something about pulling through her past. I read it and it was literally a window into a side of her life I never imagined could be real. On the surface, everything was perfect for her. But in reality, she had gone through a nasty divorce before marrying her current husband, and she had dealt with a major illness and almost lost her life. *She almost died!* Without giving too many details, let's just say this girl had gone through her share of shit. I actually fell even more in love with her blog and her story, because she was a true testament to the fact that you can accomplish anything – no matter what's thrown in your path. My "jealousy" turned into respect and compassion, and it was a total reality check for me to see that nobody ever really has it made. We're all human and we all have to deal with ups and downs.

We live in a world where everyone's lives are on display. With the advent of things like Facebook and Twitter, people are compelled to tell the story of their life online. Every single day. Social media does have wonderful purposes (I credit it for giving me the privilege of connecting with so many of you wonderful women), but it can also be a very dangerous place. Do you really think people are going to talk about how miserable they are, or how shitty their husband is on Facebook? Absolutely not. They're going to tell you how *fabulous* their life is! And how *amazing* their husband is! And how *perfect* their children are, and how their kids never cry and sleep right on through the night. They're going to post photos of their jaunts around the world, and go on and on about their promotions and their hot dates and their big houses.

Now don't get me wrong, some of what they post is probably true. We all have wins. And it's totally fine to pat yourself on the back for that promotion, or gloat about how great your kid is, or how much you love date nights with your hubby. But that's not all life is about. There is heartbreak, there is stress, there is illness, and there are losses – *huge* losses. The trick is realizing that everyone experiences life from all angles, even if they don't always talk about it. We all have our ups and downs, and if someone pretends they don't, they're full of shit.

Because people's lives are on display at all times, it's easy to get caught up in the comparison game. I've done it myself. Do you know how many times I've looked at another writer, or another life coach, and thought – *Damn, she's got it going on.* Those moments have been followed by a total frenzy of panic where I start evaluating my own brand and business, and start making lists and spreadsheets and rattling off timelines about when I'll get things done. And that's all well and good, if you can leave that anxiety out of the equation. Once you allow yourself to enter freak-out mode, you lose all control. Those lists and spreadsheets and thoughts mean nothing because they aren't about you – they're about that other chick that's got it going on.

Get Her Scoop

There's a method to the madness, however. It's totally healthy – in fact I think it's smart – to observe people who have what you want. If you can zero in on what works for them and how they achieved that success, then you are on the right track. The next time you find yourself admiring someone else's life, I want you to try this: eliminate the emotion. Stop the pity party, ditch the gossip, and look at their strategy. Figure out what they are doing right. Quick. The worst thing you can do is sit around seething over someone else's success. Where is that going to get you, aside from raising your blood pressure (and making you look really pathetic)? Jealousy is just an ugly, ugly quality. Avoid it at all costs.

Emulate your "competition" by honing
in on her secrets to success and making them
a part of your game plan.

Instead of brooding over how great her business is, flip the script. Emulate your "competition" by honing in on her secrets to success and making them a part of your game plan. Maybe she's got a knack for networking? Take note and start networking too. Take her out for coffee and ask her questions about her business. People love to talk about themselves, so I can pretty much bet she will love telling you all about her experiences and even share some expert tips and tricks with you.

The secret is learning from those you admire. Erase the word "bitch" from your vocabulary and start to look at these women as mentors. Let them be your guiding light to getting that very same life you envy.

Where there is passion, there are possibilities.

And ladies, the excuses? Not going to fly here. Sure, we don't all live in the same city or have the same backgrounds or bank account balances, but using an excuse as a crutch as why you can't achieve your dreams is a total cop-out. And thinking the people who achieved their dreams were "lucky" is the most lame excuse I've ever heard. Do you really want to be that powerless? Where there is passion, there are possibilities. It just may take a little bit longer for some of us to get there than others.

Jealousy is the *ugliest* when it comes to dieting. Am I right? Oh, how we hate on the thin girls! And even worse – the former bigger girls who are now thin girls. But you know what? There's a lot to learn there. Maybe your best friend is losing weight. You know she looks amazing, and while it's easy to get frustrated and jealous, pay attention to what she's doing. Maybe she's been hitting the gym hard and that's what helped her drop those last ten pounds. Maybe she bought that weird kettle bell thing and she's got some killer secret moves that have helped sculpt her ass. Instead of staring creepily at her vacation photos on Facebook while you inhale doughnuts, ask her if you can work out together and take note of what she's doing right. Try some of her work-outs and see how they feel for you. Allow her success to catapult your own.

Share in Her Success

As women, we are guilty of being catty. It's just a fact, and don't pretend you don't do it. We all talk shit. Some more than others, but we've all dished our fair share of gossip. Sometimes, we wrap it up in a pretty bow and call it our opinions and feelings on someone else's life. Whatever you want to disguise it as, the fact of the matter is, we all talk. And talking about other people is human nature, but it can go too far.

I've made an attempt to compliment women who I admire, rather than bitch about them, and I can't even begin to tell you how good it feels. Giving a genuine compliment to another person can do wonders for not only them, but for you as well. It just makes you feel all warm and fuzzy inside. I call it soul food. I don't know about you, but my soul is pretty damn hungry, so I try to nourish her as often as possible.

But keep in mind the compliments need to be honest. You can't just go around walking up to every woman on the street and tell her you love her shoes. That's insincere and it'll show – especially if she's wearing ugly shoes (I kid!). I'm talking honest applause from the heart. Maybe your co-worker just killed it in a meeting. Tell her. See a stranger in a really awesome outfit on the train? Let her know. I've done it before and it really does make someone's day.

Being kind is a great way to perk up your mood. Think about

how good it feels to do something nice for someone. Even if you're in the funkiest of funks, and you wind up making someone feel good, I can guarantee that you'll instantly feel better, too.

Do you know how amazing I feel when a reader emails me and tells me how much my Champagne Diet blog means to them? I feel blessed to have a brand out there that people can relate to, and for each compliment I receive I feel even more inspired to give one back. I've sent countless notes and emails to women all around the world that I am inspired by. It's like a chain reaction of kindness and it is so much more chic than hating on anyone. Confident women aren't afraid to dish out the good stuff.

And the opposite is true, too. Misery loves company. If you find yourself so filled with resentment and jealousy, chances are you may start projecting that on others. And you don't want to go there. Ever have a day where you're so pissed off that you just want to bring everyone down with you in one fell swoop? Someone else has something you want, and you're not in the mood to compliment them. You are too focused on being angry, and nothing is going to shake that feeling. Lord knows I've been there, and it's a sad place to be. But you can turn it around. You have to really stop and think about where it's going to get you. Is ruining someone else's day that fulfilling? You're better than that, baby.

Give Yourself Props!

It's especially easy to get caught up in the comparison game when it feels like everything is going wrong. Do you ever have one of those days, weeks – even months – where it feels like you can do nothing right? You know you're working your ass off, and doing your absolute best, but nothing is going as planned. So how do you shake it off and keep going? How do you not look around at everyone else who is getting through the day with a smile on their face, feeling totally accomplished, and not hate every bit of their being?

Start by applauding yourself for the things you have accomplished. I've worked with women who are so damn hard on themselves, and when I actually spell out all of the amazing things they've already achieved, they are in awe. Sometimes it really takes listing all of your wins in order to give yourself credit. We get so wrapped up in our daily lives and in the minutiae of day-to-day tasks that we fail to really see just how much ass we are already kicking.

Maybe you're stuck at a weight loss plateau. You're hitting the gym five times a week, your food plans are flawless, yet you can't seem to get rid of those last five or six pounds. Suddenly, they become an obsession. You start skipping dinner to try and get the scale to budge. Or, you go the total opposite route and just start pigging the fuck out because you've given up all hope. It's bad news and will literally destroy you. I've been on both sides of the fence.

Instead, try focusing on all the healthy rituals you've incorporated into your life. Think about how you've learned to eat like a goddess, putting only the best into your body and treating it with the utmost respect. Focus on how you've stepped up your workout game and you can not only get through an hour on the treadmill, but you feel amazing after doing so.

Jealousy is time consuming, exhausting, and gross. It's a one way ticket to misery. Steer clear of this nasty quality and let yourself shine. Celebrate your own success and the success of those around you. Ditch the anger. Be kind. Look at those who are achieving greatness and make them your mentors. And don't forget: someone else's success takes absolutely nothing away from yours. There is more than enough sparkle to go around.

Indulge YOUR BODY

CHAPTER 5
Healthy IS THE NEW SKINNY

"Women should be measured by the lives
we lead; not the size we wear."
– *Elizabeth Patch*

Here's a newsflash ladies! We cannot hide what's going on upstairs. If we're stressed, anxious, nervous or depressed, you can bet your ass it's going to show – on your ass. So in order to really sparkle, it's crucial that we learn to love ourselves and our bodies.

As a wellness expert, I have witnessed firsthand the massive connection between mind and body. I have been all over the map when it comes to size. I've been chunky, I've been thin, I've been in between, and I've been struggling with it my whole damn life. And it's always been a direct correlation to what was happening in my life at the time.

And I'm not alone. More than 40% of women in the U.S. are unhappy with their bodies. That number is staggering! I am so sick of all of us moping around, eating frozen diet dinners and feeling like less of a person because we aren't 115 pounds. That attitude does not fly in this champagne makeover, and I'll tell you why.

Living an effervescent life means feeling fabulous. And you can't fake the funk. Fabulous is an aura that you exude when you actually believe it. Feeling fabulous has little to do with appearance, and everything to do with attitude. And fabulous and unhealthy are like oil and water – they just don't mix.

Think about this: if you ate a giant meal at Wendy's, put on sweatpants, and didn't brush your teeth, and you went around saying you felt fabulous, it would never work. But let's flip the script. If you ate a delicious meal, let's say a filet mignon with a side of roasted red potatoes and sautéed spinach, and you paired it with a crisp glass of sparkling wine, and you wore your absolute hottest outfit, how would you feel? You'd feel like a million dollars and *that* is what this lifestyle is all about.

Now, I know what you're thinking. You're probably all like: *There's no way in hell I can actually feel sexy and glamorous when I'm carrying around an extra fifty pounds.* But that could not be further from the truth. I'm not telling you to go on an extreme diet; I'm also not telling you to keep eating yourself into oblivion and convince yourself it's okay. I am telling you to change your attitude and the choices you make, and I can assure you you'll start to look smoking hot. By making small changes, like swapping out Twinkies for let's say, yogurt, and doing more things that make you happy, you will start to see results. Your skin will glow, you'll smile more, and you'll feel like a new woman. I promise.

A couple of years ago, I was in a rut. I was working crazy hours, and had zero time for the gym, let alone worrying about counting calories. I had put on a couple pounds and I felt terrible. Because I felt terrible, I stopped getting my weekly manicures. So now I was feeling large and in charge, and I had crappy nails. Why on earth would I feel like getting my hair done if I was bloated with crappy nails? So, I stopped that too. See how quickly it all spirals?

But I took charge, and went and got a manicure one Sunday afternoon. I picked out the brightest, loudest shade of red I could find. I never go for red, but I felt like I had to spice things up. So, there I was, sucking in my muffin top, getting my nails done, and feeling far from beautiful. But as soon as my manicure was over, something came over me. I felt sexier. I stood taller. I think I even strutted a little. Manicures were always something I did when I was feeling healthy and hot, so having one done brought me back to that mental place almost instantly.

Afterward, I went to the supermarket. Instead of picking up chips, I got fruit. I went home, lounged in my favorite pretty pajamas, and admired my long, red, out-of-character, but-oh-so-diva-like nails. Eventually, I got my butt back into the gym and knocked off those fifteen pounds, but it took time. And a lot of manicures.

So, if you're feeling unmotivated, I want you to try something. Choose one thing that makes you feel glamorous. Maybe it's buying a really pretty pair of pajamas and lounging in them with a full face of makeup and marabou slippers (think Marilyn). Maybe it's a luxurious bubble bath with scented bath oils. Maybe it's going for a boxing lesson. Maybe it's discovering a new recipe and cooking yourself a delicious dinner. It doesn't have to be fancy, or expensive. It just has to make you feel beautiful.

Curve Appeal

Luckily, the world is catching on to the fact that beauty does not mean we should see your ribs in a bikini. In June 2011, *Vogue* Italia did a spread featuring plus-sized models Tara Lynn, Candice Huffine and Robyn Lawley. The cover featured the three models in lingerie, sitting at a table with plates filled with pasta and glasses of red wine (yum!). The caption "Belle Vere" was painted across the photograph, which means "true beauty" in Italian. *Vogue*. Magazine. *Vogue*! The most elite fashion magazine in the world featured *real* women. I can't tell you how elated this made me.

Inside the magazine were absolutely stunning photographs of the three women, all in black and white, traipsing through a hotel in next to nothing. Thighs out, boobs out, butts out, for the entire fashion world to see. These voluptuous beauties were not only breathtaking; they rocked the media headlines for weeks thereafter, and in the best way possible.

I remember when I first saw the cover. My heart skipped a beat and I actually said out loud, "Finally." I felt proud and excited that these hot mamas were getting the attention they deserved. They were pioneers for women everywhere who don't, and most often can't, conform to the unrealistic goals magazines and movies set for us.

Weeks after that issue of *Vogue* came out, Twitter and Facebook were all buzzing about how radiantly gorgeous these women were. Men and women alike were blown away by the confidence of these women that beamed out through the pages of the magazine. Because of the magnitude of that issue, the tides have turned in the way the media views women. It's a long road, but we are getting there slowly.

Living an effervescent life truly is about "belle vere." It's about indulging in the things you love and enjoying life. It's about muting all the negative thoughts in your head, forgetting that your crazy ex-boyfriend ever called you fat, and loving that powerful, glamorous woman deep inside.

Living an effervescent life truly is about "belle vere." It's about indulging in the things you love and enjoying life. It's about muting all the negative thoughts in your head, forgetting that your crazy ex-boyfriend ever called you fat, and loving that powerful, glamorous woman deep inside. She's in there; you just have to let her out. I don't care how many rolls you have, how much cellulite is on your thighs, or how those jeans from when you were twenty-two don't fit anymore. Champagne Girls make it work. They celebrate it all.

Does this Diet Make my Ass Look Big?

Are you as sick as I am of articles, talk shows and books filled with people telling you to give everything up that you love in order to live a healthy life? I have yet to find a diet that really works for me, and I've yet to connect with anyone who tells me I can eat four almonds as a snack. And I want to shove a martini down the throat of anyone who tells me I can't drink if I want to be skinny and tell them to loosen up.

I am no stranger to diets. I have struggled with my weight and body image pretty much since I came flying out of the womb. I am certain that I was born with an addiction to Chips Ahoy (the classic ones, not the chewy kind), and I can remember feeling "fat" as young as seven. This is what inspired me to start coaching other women on wellness. I wanted to learn as much as I could about why we have emotional attachments to food, and how we can form better relationships with our bodies. And, guess what? *It is* possible.

I was obsessed with food from a young age. There were not many second-graders who fantasized about retirement, but I was one of them. I was jealous of my grandmother because I, too, wanted to stay home all day and eat cake. My grandma had the life, in my eyes. Pound cake and tea while watching Oprah re-runs? That sure beat out dodgeball in my book.

Year after year, diet after diet, I always found myself back at the same place – miserable, and even heavier than I was before I started each diet. If I had to look at one more box of low-fat cookies or count one more point, I was certain my head would explode. I tried every diet plan under the sun: Atkins, Jenny Craig, Weight Watchers, The South Beach Diet, low-carb diets – all of it. The results I got were often quick, but fleeting. I'd lose weight, but I'd also be zapped of all my energy, and I looked pale and unhealthy. Before I knew it, I was frustrated and bored with whatever regimen I was on, and the weight came right back on.

Each time I'd go off one of my diets, it was party time! I'd celebrate by binging on my favorite junk food. Diets were actually making me fatter.

And I'm sure I'm not alone here. More than two-thirds of adults are overweight. Americans are generally unhealthy and 95% of people who go on diets fail. They wind up gaining back whatever weight they lost, because diets are completely unrealistic. Nobody can go around equating their food into point systems, or living off boxed diet dinners forever. So we go on diets, lose weight, gain it back, and go on diets again. It's no wonder diet companies are multi-million dollar businesses.

As I mentioned in the introduction, the first time I really learned how to eat well was after Liron, a coworker and good friend at MTV broke it down for me. She promised me that if I just ate whole, nutritious, "real" food, I'd be able to lose weight and get healthy without ever counting another calorie, point, or fat gram again. I was extremely skeptical of her plan, but decided that I'd give it a shot. At the time, I was fat, desperate, and miserable. Tied up in an emotionally-draining relationship and working long hours did a number on my system, and there was nothing more comforting than coming home at the end of a long day and going to town on a large pizza and Coors Light (see the connection?). I shudder when I think about how truly disgusting my eating habits were, but thankful that I put a kibosh on it before things got too out of hand.

I began to do my own research on eating whole foods, including fresh vegetables, fruit, whole grains and proteins such as beans, tofu and lean meats in the form of chicken or turkey. I'm not one to preach about what you should or shouldn't eat when it comes to meat, but I will say this: if you do choose to eat meat, please pay attention to where your meat is coming from. USDA certified organic only, and make sure it is all hormone and antibiotic-free. If you eat red meat, please keep it to a very minimal amount. Recent studies have shown that the consumption of red meat, especially processed meat (think fast food, most restaurant meat, non-USDA certified organic) is directly related to premature death and cancer.

I started following a whole foods diet and gave up processed foods. I said goodbye to preservatives and all of the junk I was used to eating, and I stopped counting calories or fat grams. Instead, I started reading nutrition labels. I made sure if I ate something out of a box or a bag, it was preservative-free and made from natural ingredients only. My rule of thumb for ingredient listings was: if I can't pronounce it, I can't eat it.

There are exceptions, of course. I told you I was Italian! We love our food. If I want something, I don't deprive myself. If I want a cupcake, I eat it. Maybe I'll eat half of it on a good day. I just don't binge on seventeen cupcakes at once. You can't go crazy. It's really pretty logical.

But it wasn't just about the food. I revamped my lifestyle as well. I worked my tits off to get into a better position at my job and eventually I landed a promotion. I said goodbye to long hours. I also finally said goodbye to that relationship. Everything was falling into place.

Not only did I lose some weight, but my hair became shinier and my skin glowed. I had more energy than ever, and my mood was instantly boosted. I was happy. Because I felt better, I also took on a new attitude about weight loss. I wasn't determined to lose X amount of pounds anymore, instead it was about putting the best foods in my body and treating it with respect. In addition, I also learned to treat *myself* with respect. I realized how unhealthy I was – both physically and emotionally – and how poorly I had treated myself for years. I was now in control of my life and my health, and it felt amazing.

And the best part was I didn't have to give up the things I loved. I don't know about you, but I adore a nice big glass of wine (or three) on a Friday night, and I allow myself to have it. Life is about balance, not deprivation and torture. Following restrictive diets are a recipe for disaster. They aren't long-term solutions. Nobody is going to stay on Jenny Craig forever. And why would you want to? The freedom in eating sensibly is wonderful. Knowing that you can walk into a restaurant and make smart choices off the menu and really understand what you're putting in your body rather than relying on pre-made entrees or a plate of lettuce is pretty liberating.

You have the ability to control the
way you eat, think and live.

So if you're feeling frustrated about your weight, please know that you are in complete control. There is a wealth of knowledge available to you so that you can educate yourself about your body and about food. You have the ability to control the way you eat, think and live. How's that for empowering?

The "F" Word

How many times have you called yourself fat? The sentence "I feel fat" has probably been muttered hundreds of times more than "I feel gorgeous" over the course of my lifetime. Isn't that sad?

Negative self-talk is more detrimental than you probably realize. Studies show that engaging in "fat talk" increases our risk for depression. And guess what? Calling ourselves fat is even worse than the media calling women fat, according to research. Now, *that's* scary.

Old habits die hard, and even though we'd love to never use the "F" word again, it might be difficult. So how about this: every time you catch yourself judging your body and referring to yourself as fat, try immediately complimenting yourself afterward. So, for example, if you get dressed for a party and look in the mirror and find yourself saying, "I look fat!" find something you love about yourself and say it out loud. "I have gorgeous eyes," or "Damn, my ass looks great!" will do the trick. I do it all the time as a way to dig myself out of the rabbit hole when I start obsessively staring at myself in the mirror and picking apart every imperfection. When I feel a panic attack coming on, I compliment myself on my hair, which happens to be quite fabulous. There, I said it. I love my hair. It's long, blonde and pin straight. My "skinny" friends tease me that they're envious of it, and to that I say – you can't have it all, bitch. I may have a couple extra pounds to work with, but I've got damn good hair.

Figure out whatever it is that you love about yourself, and proclaim it. You may giggle, but trust me on this one, ladies. Let's kick the "F" word to the curb, once and for all.

So let's recap, shall we? We are no longer going to obsess over the scale. We're going to say goodbye to fad diets, because they just don't work. Instead, we're going to focus on eating whole, nutritious foods. And most importantly – we're going to love every lump, bump and curve that we've got. Because if we don't start embracing these bods, who will? There isn't one other person on the planet that should validate us except us. Now can I get an Amen?

CHAPTER 6
LET'S GET *Physical*

"If you really want to do something, you'll find a
way. If you don't, you'll find an excuse."
– Jim Rohn

Want to know the quickest way to get motivated to work
out? Imagine not being physically able to. I will never forget
what it felt like to not be able to walk. To not have the muscle
strength to physically put one leg in front of the other was one
of the scariest feelings I've ever experienced.

Let me back track. It was the summer of 2004, Labor Day
weekend to be exact. I had just gotten past the "Chuck Goldenfuck incident," so I was jobless. To top it off, I had been limping
around for the better part of the summer, positive that I had just
pulled a muscle and it would heal itself. Unemployed and unable
to walk didn't exactly do wonders for my confidence. I certainly
was not at my best, that's for sure.

Each morning I'd wake up, hoping I'd feel better, but the pain
seemed to be getting worse. Finally, when it had gotten so bad
that I could no longer stand, I went to my doctor. She was unable
to tell what was wrong with me without doing an MRI or x-ray,
and because of the holiday, most Orthopedist offices were closed.
She sent me home and told me to get crutches while I waited to
see a specialist.

Fast forward two weeks later; I was finally able to get an appointment with an Orthopedist who ordered me to see a physical therapist. By this point, I had been off my right leg for so long
that it was noticeably thinner than the left (*attractive*, really). The
muscle mass had decreased so much from being on crutches and

I was for a lack of a better term – screwed.

After an examination, it was determined that I had strained my hip flexors; a group of muscles that run from the back of the lower spine to the front of the thigh. This injury is common in professional athletes, so the fact that I had somehow achieved a pro-sports injury was pretty hilarious, considering the only physical activity I was fond of was shopping. To this day I have no idea how I did this to myself, but I'm assuming it involved taking a few drunken spills in five-inch heels.

I'd have to report to physical therapy three times per week, endure excruciating exercises to heal my muscles, and eventually, learn how to walk again. I was given a cane (yes, a cane, but you know I rocked it like a diva), and I had to make peace with the fact that this office would be my new home for the next few months. If it wasn't for my therapist's ball-busting sense of humor, I don't know what I would have done. From my first appointment, where he told the waiting room I had hurt my leg from dancing on a bar, I knew I'd met my match. Barry would tease all his patients, and the entire office would be roaring with laughter when most of us would have otherwise been in tears. He kept our mind off our problems and kept us focused on the positive. We were all there to get better; some of us had injuries that would eventually heal, and others would never be fully rehabilitated, but we were all motivated to be our absolute best.

When I'm too lazy to exercise, I remind
myself of how lucky I am that I *can* exercise.
I remind myself of how blessed I am that I have
the ability to get on that treadmill.

After three months of rigorous training to get back on my feet, the day came where I was finally able to walk without a cane. Barry waited for me across the room, arms outstretched, as if I were a toddler as he told me to walk toward him. I literally put one foot in front of the other, stared straight ahead, and walked. I may have wobbled a bit, but I was back on my feet. It was one of the best days of my life.

After that experience, I vowed to never take my body or my health for granted ever again. You don't know what you've got till it's gone, and let me tell you; not being able to walk puts everything in perspective. I had a new lease on life. I joined the gym and started working out on a regular basis. Though it's been eight years since my injury, I remind myself of that summer all the time. When I'm too lazy to exercise, I remind myself of how lucky I am that I *can* exercise. I remind myself of how blessed I am that I have the ability to get on that treadmill. I remind myself of how blessed I am to even be able to walk to the gym. When you have your health, you have everything.

Good health is something we need to maintain, and working out is one of the best ways to keep it in check. Everything from cancer prevention and cutting your risk of heart disease, to avoiding stroke and living longer are listed among the reasons you should get up off your ass and move. Not to mention being fit and energized. And I'm game for anything that will guarantee me a healthy life – preferably one that's nice and long.

What's In It for Me?

If you ever needed a reason to get in that gym, it's this: studies now show that regular exercise can reduce your risk of developing Alzheimer's disease. Physical activity – whether it's cardio or resistance training – can keep that brain of yours sharp and help you avoid going bat shit crazy. I don't know about you, but I will gladly devote twenty minutes a day to an elliptical trainer if I can guarantee I'll know my own name when I'm seventy.

And what's even more mind-blowing, physical activity can actually grow the brain of an adult. Research shows that adults between the ages of sixty and eighty who walked moderately for thirty to forty-five minutes three days per week showed a 2% growth in the hippocampus region of their brain, which is the area responsible for memory. Another study showed that resistance training in adults improved thinking and memory, which is great news for someone who dreads their cardio (ahem). Aerobic activity also improves sleep and reduces stress, two things that are crucial for maintaining brain health and a sharp mind.

In addition to the mental benefits of exercise, working out on a regular basis also plays a huge role in cutting your risk of developing cancer. And the great news is you don't have to spend hours in the gym to reap the benefits. Studies show that just thirty minutes of moderate exercise per day cuts your cancer risk by 30% to 50%. That number is huge!

And don't forget your heart. Daily exercise can help prevent heart disease and stroke by strengthening your heart muscle, lowering your blood pressure, raising your good cholesterol and lowering bad cholesterol, improving blood flow, and increasing your heart's working capacity. Honestly, do I need to keep going? So bust a move ladies, and set yourself up for a long, healthy life.

Every Little Step

Now that we know how beneficial it is to work out regularly, let's address something: what the hell are we supposed to be doing? What constitutes "regular exercise" anyway? Is it me, or does everything we read makes us feel like we should be running marathons in order to benefit from a workout? Articles that suggest we need to spend an hour a day running, doing hundreds of crunches, or working out with a personal trainer make most of want to throw in the towel before we even begin. While it's crucial to dedicate at least twenty minutes per day to a regular workout routine to maintain good health, the truth is – every little bit counts. Our bodies need movement throughout the day. Even if you hit the gym, you've gotta keep it going all day long. There are so many small ways in which we can incorporate movement; whether it's pacing while you're on the phone, cleaning the house, going for walks to the store, or doing squats while watching television. Being as active as possible will help burn calories and get your blood pumping. Rather than viewing exercise as something that's incredibly time-intensive, think about it as getting in as much physical activity as possible each day, even if it's a little bit at a time.

Finding Your MOET-ivation

And don't forget, every step we take is a calorie burned, and a glass of bubbly earned! I may encourage wellness and healthy living, but Lord knows I love my wine and pasta. I'm Italian, remember? I am not about starvation and deprivation. But that means I need to burn off the excess calories I'm putting in my body. So if you like to indulge in the finer things in life (like say, a block of cheddar cheese or an extra glass or three of wine on the weekends), you'd better get moving. We have to balance out our lifestyles. And I don't know about you, but I'll surely sweat for an extra half hour to ensure that I can have my wine when I want it.

Whether it's fitting into that bikini, or allowing yourself to indulge in a glass of champagne, we all need something that will motivate us to move. My motivations change from time to time, and they range from anything like trying out my new workout gear, to clearing my head, to sparking my creativity. In fact, whenever I experienced writer's block with this book, I'd hit the gym for a quick run and the words came pouring out of me. It was my saving grace.

And don't forget, every step we take is a
calorie burned, and a glass of bubbly earned!

Working out brings a whole new element into my life. It provides me with precious Me Time, it boosts my mood, and it makes me feel more confident. Sometimes my motivation is just getting some alone time to clear my head after a long, stressful day at work and escape "the real world."

The gym culture can be invigorating too, and it's the main reason I haven't ditched my membership for at-home workout DVD's (although I do love a good old fashioned Jane Fonda workout, I must admit – belted leotards anyone?) Even if I haven't worked out in a month, the minute I step foot in the gym, I feel better. Just being around other people who are motivated to be fit makes me feel like I'm one of them. And let's be honest, a little healthy competition never hurt anyone. If I see a hot chick running on a treadmill next to me, you bet your ass it's going to make me want to run, too. Even if I'm sweating my boobs off and gasping for air, I *will* keep up with those around me.

It's important to make sure you're doing a workout you enjoy. I try so hard to love Spin class, but I just can't get into it. Maybe it's the fact that everyone around me seems like they've just competed in the *Tour de France*, complete with their spandex biker shorts and fancy iPod arm bands. It's just way too serious for me. And don't get me started on the instructors. Those Janet Jackson style hands-free microphones that they shout commands into make me incredibly uneasy. But to each her own! It's all about what works for you.

So, remember ladies, physical activity is crucial to living an effervescent, sparkling life. We need to keep our beautiful bodies in motion so that we can ward off disease and stay fit and energized. And it's not supposed to be torture! Move as much as possible, and choose workouts that fit with your lifestyle. And the next time you're less than excited to workout, think about all of the fabulous benefits in store for you, think about how lucky you are that you can work out – and most importantly, do what works for you.

CHAPTER 7
Self-Indulgence CAN SAVE YOUR LIFE

"I restore myself when I'm alone."
– *Marilyn Monroe*

Now that we're knee-deep in your sparkling, champagne makeover, I want to reiterate one very important point: this lifestyle is about celebrating yourself! And to truly celebrate every piece of your being, you're going to need to learn to self-indulge. That's right – say it with me ladies – self-indulge.

Contrary to what the world tells us, self-indulgence is not a dirty term. For some reason, our society has taught us that being a martyr is just what you do as a woman. We all sing that "woe is me" song as we keep piling more shit on our plates. We're told that "Me Time" is synonymous with being selfish. Well you know what? I think it's a load of crap. Who made these rules up, anyway? It's time to rewrite the book – fast.

Don't get me wrong, things need to get done. Someone has to pay the rent, right? We can't throw caution to the wind and quit our jobs or stop being functional adults. But we also have to recharge, revive and reset our batteries because we want to sparkle, not burn out. And there is a huge difference between the two.

When I talk about self-indulging, I'm not just talking about taking candlelit bubble baths with your favorite glass (or bottle) of wine – although that is a fabulous way to unwind. But something as simple as a morning walk can do wonders for your brain and your body. Setting aside Me Time is just as necessary as paying the bills and going to work. And life is hectic, so you'll need to get creative with your ideas and your time. But trust me

– once you see how amazing it feels to spend some quality time with yourself, you'll be sure to mark a regular space for it in your calendar.

In my coaching practice, I find that the number one thing my clients are looking for is balance in their lives. And here's the first thing I tell people: balance is a myth. You should either do something with gusto, or don't do it at all. You are doing yourself and those around you a disservice if you're trying to juggle two things at once. For example, if I take work home with me, I am sacrificing precious time with my husband by not giving him my full attention. If I've worked my ass off all week, and we're finally together for a romantic dinner, but I'm half focused on my Blackberry and half in a conversation with him that is not balance. That's a poor attempt at multi-tasking that will just leave him frustrated, and my work sloppy.

The concept of balance is a reminder that we should be living a well-rounded life. We can't be all work all the time, and we can't be all play all the time, either. We need to make sure that whatever area we're focusing on in the moment; we're giving it our all.

The concept of balance is a reminder that we should be living a well-rounded life. We can't be all work all the time, and we can't be all play all the time, either. We need to make sure that whatever area we're focusing on in the moment; we're giving it our all. So when it comes to making time for yourself, make sure you really "in it." That means, no phone, no Twitter, no Facebook, no obligations: just you. Commit. Indulge. Enjoy. You deserve nothing less.

Be Selfish, Be Healthy

The benefits of Me Time go far beyond feeling like you can actually think straight. Living effervescently means living fully, happily and healthily. There are numerous health benefits that come into play when you start taking care of yourself and your body. Did you know something as simple as a good night's sleep can actually help prevent disease? Chronic sleep deprivation and exhaustion causes a release of stress hormones, which causes your blood sugar to rise, in turn heightening your risk of diabetes and heart disease. Scary stuff, huh? Plus, sleeping well does wonders for your skin and also aids in weight loss. Double bonus.

Exercise is another great way to get some Me Time in, and it also obviously provides great health benefits. But here's one rule: you must eliminate the notion that working out is punishment. So many of us tell ourselves "I'll eat this doughnut and just run an extra twenty minutes at the gym!" That's the worst logic because it connects exercise to a negative experience. If you can learn to view working out as a way to indulge in a little alone time, then you're golden. And the benefits you'll reap are invaluable. Regular exercise, as you know, does wonders for the mind and body and is truly the ticket to avoiding a nervous breakdown.

All of this is not to freak you out and make you book a week's vacation at a spa retreat (although, I won't stop you. And will you invite me?) I'm telling you this so that you start taking control of your life and your health. And of course it's all the more reason to start treating yourself like a queen!

Just Say No

I am the first to admit I have always been a people pleaser. I love to nurture and take care of others, and nothing makes me smile more than making someone happy. And that's all fine and dandy if you can separate other people's happiness from your own, and realize that ultimately your happiness is your primary responsibility.

Think about when you're getting ready to take off on an airplane. You know that mind-numbing safety announcement that comes on, the one that we've all learned to ignore? Well if you really pay attention it has a much deeper meaning that you probably realize. The flight attendants tell us to put our own oxygen mask on before helping anyone else. Why? Because if we're dead, we can't save another person. Duh! It's really so simple, yet so profound, and it applies to every single area of our day to day lives. If you help everyone else around you before you help yourself, you're setting yourself up to die. Or at least be really unhappy.

I see this happen time and time again, especially in relationships. So many women think that putting their man first is the key to a healthy romance. Think again, ladies! Sure, it's great to take care of your man, cook him dinners, consider his feelings and all that jazz. But at the end of the day, you have to make your happiness a priority or the whole damn thing is destined to fail. It's all about walking that fine line, which can be tricky at times. Just remember this: if you're miserable, there's no way in hell that relationship stands a chance.

I love being left alone with my thoughts,
reflecting upon everything, and just embracing the
tranquil moments that you can only really achieve
when you're by yourself.

It's also important to give yourself a permission slip to just "shut off" sometimes. Ever have that annoying girlfriend who keeps calling you until you pick up? Her boyfriend is breaking up with her for the sixteenth time and she just *needs* to talk to you. Or maybe you've got a sky-high pile of laundry that you can literally smell from the next room. I don't care how much these things are nagging you, when you're stressed and exhausted, it's okay to say no. Grab a cocktail and chill out. Life coach's orders! That girlfriend, that pile of laundry – it'll all be there when you're strong enough to deal with it. If you're not feeling it, just say no. Your body and your brain will thank you.

Flying Solo

One of my favorite things to do is take myself out on dates. I find so much solace in going out to dinner and enjoying a delicious meal and a glass of wine all alone. To some it may seem weird or antisocial, but hey – I like myself! And I happen to think it's one of the most peaceful things in the world to do. I love being left alone with my thoughts, reflecting upon everything, and just embracing the tranquil moments that you can only really achieve when you're by yourself. If it's not a dinner date, I often take myself window shopping or for a pedicure.

I crave these solo rendezvous because it gives me a chance to do some bonding with who I am at the core. It gives me a chance to survey what's going on upstairs and make changes if necessary. I get to catch up with my thoughts that get buried underneath the business meetings, conference calls and O.P.P.'s (Other People's Priorities). It allows me take my soul's temperature and make sure she's doing okay.

The next time you find yourself feeling burnt; promise me you'll give this a whirl. Even if its thirty minutes at a coffee shop, go it alone, your self will thank you.

Little Luxuries

I know you're probably sitting here thinking, "all of this is great, but I have no time for myself!" Well, that is bullshit. Yes, you heard me – bullshit! There is always time for you. Like I mentioned earlier, depending on your budget and your calendar, you're going to have to put on your thinking tiara and get creative with ways to indulge, but trust me, there are ways.

For those of us that have more flexible schedules, and bank accounts, then by all means, go crazy, sister. I'm not saying you should dish out thousands of dollars on a lavish wardrobe and celebrity hairstylists and be completely irresponsible with your finances, but keeping up with your beauty rituals is so important – on any budget. Things that may seem shallow and unimportant at times really are so crucial to your well-being. If you go for regular manicures, hair appointments, shopping trips, massages, whatever – keep doing it. Don't let your routine suffer just because you're busy. You can find the time to squeeze it in if you prioritize. Studies show that people who look good feel good. Nobody can be happy if they look like a disheveled slob. Am I right? If you're skimping on your regular routine, you'll run the risk of feeling depressed and it'll get harder and harder to treat yourself.

And don't feel guilty about this stuff, either. Research shows that 96% of women feel guilty for *something* on a daily basis. And 80% of women feel bad spending money on themselves. If you work hard, you deserve to responsibly reap the rewards. Want a massage? Can you afford it without skipping your electric bill that month? Then go for it. And enjoy every damn second.

If you're in the majority of the population where money and time is tight (hello?), then have no fear. There are plenty of ways you can pamper yourself on a dime. I'm a huge fan of at-home spa nights. There is nothing more I love than discount shopping for as many beauty products that I can spring for, buying a cheap bottle of wine, whipping out my favorite bath robe, and going to town. I don't know if it's a kind of nostalgia I get from revisiting the entire line of Sally Hansen nail products, or slapping on one of those old school St. Ive's green facial masks, but I absolutely adore girlifying myself on a Friday night. Traipsing around my apartment with a goblet of Chardonnay and a face mask is my idea of personal heaven.

And of course, there's the happy medium. You're not dead broke, but you're not a millionaire, and you can stand to indulge once a month. Maybe it's a massage that keeps you from losing your mind or a trip to Nordstrom that warms the cockles of your heart. Remember, indulging yourself is a necessity. Whatever it is, make sure that you're spoiling yourself at least a little bit on a regular basis. Because when that oxygen mask drops, it's every woman for herself.

CHAPTER 8
WHEN IN DOUBT, BE *Glamorous*

"Darling, the legs aren't so beautiful,
I just know what to do with them."
– *Marlene Dietrich*

Enough about the serious stuff; let's have some fun. Your champagne makeover is just as much about decking yourself out in pearls and pretty shoes as it is about establishing your rules for a happy, fulfilled life. So let's move onto to part deux, shall we? Feel free to break for a glass of bubbly for this part, I'll wait for you.

I am all girl all the way. And I suspect if you're reading this book, you are, too. I love all of the stuff that makes tomboys gag – Sex and the City, pink martinis and glitter. Faux fur! Champagne! Pretty things! And being glamorous is quite possibly one of the most fun parts of being a Champagne Girl.

Being glamorous is two-fold: it's one part glitzy, effortless elegance, and one-part attitude. Glamorous women handle everything with poise. And most importantly, they are confident. Let's look at some iconic glam ladies of the past: Marilyn Monroe sits way atop my list. She captured the true essence of glamour in a way that has lived on for decades, even well past her untimely death. She was silly, playful, undeniably sexy, and beautiful. Her charismatic personality and platinum blonde hair kept both men and women on the edge of their seats. People adored her. They still do. She is timeless beauty to the max.

And of course, Elizabeth Taylor, known for her flowing caftans and fistful of jewels. She always appeared breathtakingly beautiful, with a fashion sense like no other and a diamond collection that could blind you. She was also known for marrying and subsequently divorcing eight-hundred men, but she did it with grace. You never saw Liz melting down in public with smeared eyeliner. She never crashed cars on Sunset Boulevard or trash-talked her ex-lovers on television. As she'd say, "Pour yourself a drink, put on some lipstick, and pull yourself together." Liz knew how to do it.

And Jackie O? Need I say more?

I try really hard to channel these fabulous women as often as possible, especially when I find myself in situations where my inner Brooklyn girl wants to come out swinging. You see, I have this thing where I just can't keep my mouth shut at times. I don't know if it's because I'm a New Yorker, or I was raised by a single mother who had to fight for everything she had, but I am not into being walked on. And I'll prove to you every chance I get that I won't take shit – from anyone.

Now, don't take this the wrong way. As women, we absolutely need to stand up for ourselves and reign supreme as powerful, assertive creatures. I am a feminist just as much as the next person. But as much as that tough-as-nails attitude can really come in handy, it can also get us into trouble if not properly channeled – and that is definitely *not* glamorous.

Looking back on my youth, I sometimes cringe at some of the things I said or did when provoked (or unprovoked). I'll never forget the time it got *really* scary. I was out with a group of friends one summer night, and as we were leaving a bar, a girl purposely bumped into me and my friends with her umbrella. I barked something at her, mainly protecting my friend Jen who is about half my size, and umbrella girl fired back at me. Rather than walking away (I mean come on, how could I just let her curse me out in the middle of the street?), I fired back. Before I knew it, umbrella girl was swinging at me and little Jen, and I felt like I was in the middle of a scene from *Jersey Shore*. I quickly walked away, mortified, and promised myself that I would never,

ever channel my inner J Woww again.

From that point on, I learned to quiet my inner loud mouth. No matter how much you want to defend yourself, or your friends, it's just not worth creating a scene over. Glamorous women do not do scenes. It's tacky and it's gross. Got it?

You might be yawning right now, thinking I'm trying to convince you that should lose your flair. Au contraire, ladies! Being a glamorous does not infer that you should be stuffy. I have mastered the art of combining my fiery side with my feminine side, and I encourage women to do the same by following a few key principles as part of this champagne makeover. You can still be a brazen, ballsy bitch and be a lady. There's no need to put a sock over the fire alarm. This book is called *Sparkle*, for goodness' sake! But there's a way to do it. There are lines that need to be drawn, and mantras that must be followed. Read on, precious pearls.

Ladies Don't do Drama

While drama can be highly addictive and oh-so-juicy, try to keep it at arm's length. I personally get my dramatic rocks off by entrenching myself in endless hours of reality TV. Sure, it's sad that these people actually have the time to fight with each other all day long, but as long as I'm not the one getting vodka splashed on me, I'll remain a happy voyeur.

Whenever I work with clients who find themselves in situations where their inner bitch is being tested, the advice I give them is to use silence as a power tool. I know how hard this is, believe me. But if someone is trying to get a rise out of you, and you can manage to keep your glossed-up lips sealed, you will *scare the shit out of your opponent*. Biting your tongue, especially when dealing with an irrational person, is your best bet here and will give you the time to really collect your thoughts and then fire back with something well thought out and extra spicy. Pick your words wisely. Most of the time, crazy people aren't listening anyway.

We can't control other people, but we sure as hell can control how we deal with them.

Drama in relationships is inherently unavoidable, even the best partnerships get side-tracked by fights and daily annoyances. Nobody is perfect. So how do you stay lady-like and poised when your significant other is on your shit list? This is where that fabulous term "communication" comes into play. I know, I sound like an 80's self-help book, but it's true! Communicate, communicate, communicate. But don't do it when your blood is boiling. It's easier to curb your frustration when the problems are small. Let's say, your hubby left you a little gift on the toilet seat. That's a much smaller beast to tame than dealing with a cheater. But regardless, your response to these issues is your choice. We can't control others, but we sure as hell can control how we deal with them. Maybe you want to cut his dick off, but that won't get you anywhere, besides a jail cell (and some very bad karma). Breathe, sip, and come back to it when the dust has settled a bit.

Or, in the cheating case, cut the bastard out of your life and refrain from ever giving him the pleasure of speaking to you again. Silence is power, remember? And if you're finding it hard to keep your inner Brooklyn girl quiet, remember to breathe deeply like we talked about in the earlier chapters. Simply taking a few deep breaths will calm you down and give you a few minutes to regroup and realize that screaming profanities at your partner is probably not the best idea. For now, anyway.

Dress You Up in My Love

So now that we know how to avoid being insane, let's talk about style. Elegant ladies kill it in the wardrobe department. Listen, I'm not saying you should look like you're walking the red carpet every day, but adding a dash of glamour to your closet can only lead to good things.

This does not require a complete fashion overhaul, either. There are tons of ways to pull off an enchanting, fabulous look without going overboard. For example, jewels always make me feel glamorous. Costume jewels, specifically. Lord knows I can't afford a five carat diamond, but that doesn't mean I shouldn't wear one. Who's going to know if it's real, anyway? Wearing a giant, fun ring or a stack of jingling bangles is my go-to for sophisticated, feminine fashion. And they don't have to be expensive. I've found some of my best pieces at discount stores, flea markets – even my grandma's jewelry box.

Glamorous women don't *do* drama, but I never
said they couldn't *wear* drama.

And you just can't go wrong with color. Vibrant, flashy patterns are a signature glam look, specifically caftans or flowing, sheer fabrics. Tell me you don't feel like a million bucks in a billowing dress or long top? Bonus points if it has beading. Glamorous women don't *do* drama, but I never said they couldn't *wear* drama.

Now if I were twenty-two, I'd advise you to exclusively wear heels and burn all of your flats, immediately. When I was young, I trotted around Manhattan like a show pony in stilettos at all hours of the night. My motto was *the higher the better*. It didn't matter if it was rain, sleet or snow, I wouldn't be caught dead in season-appropriate footwear. But now that I've got ten years (and fifteen pounds) on my former stilted self, I'm here to rally for comfort. Thanks to designers like Tory Burch and Michael Kors, flats can be fashionable. And frankly, I wouldn't give a shit if my flats came from Payless, so long as they were fabulous. They key to a glamorous pair of flats is all about the embellishment. You want to make sure your shoe is functional, yet blingtastic. Jeweled flats are where it's at.

Of course, these are all simply suggestions. If you feel sexiest in Champion sweats and six inch heels, then you have to do what works for you. And if you do pair those two things together, please email me a photo. But, nonetheless, being glamorous is all about elegance and comfort. And to look elegant, you've got to feel elegant.

But it doesn't stop with dresses and jewels. Bedtime glamour is where it's at. After you're done getting frisky, if you're not comfortable passing out in the nude (I know I personally have an irrational fear of my apartment burning down at 3 am and must sleep clothed), then get acquainted with satin pajamas. Those silky pant sets are super chic, as are silk night gowns. As I mentioned earlier, I went through a dark period of my life when I only wore wine-stained Hello Kitty pajamas to bed, and let me tell you, I did not feel like a lady. The second I revamped my pajama collection was when it all clicked. There's nothing like lounging on the couch with a glass of champagne or wine in a pair of pretty PJs.

And I don't know about you, but nothing makes me feel more like sexing than putting on a lace-trimmed teddy that strategically hides my belly. Bonus points if you wear pearls with it. Lace and silk may feel a little Danielle Steele, but let me tell you, they up the glam factor like nobody's business (and they provide great coverage!) Think about old Hollywood films. Screen sirens of yesteryear never ran around in nipple clamps and ball gags (at least not on camera). They were always floating around in some kind of sexy little "number." Vintage inspired lingerie is the best, in my opinion. Think silk slips over crotchless panties.

And keep in mind, this is all in good fun. Whether you're draped in beautiful fabrics or you're hanging out in a tank top and ripped jeans, you'll look your best when you're comfortable. You should wear, and act, however you feel best. The sexiest women are the most confident woman. So raise your glass and rock it out, ladies. Make me proud.

Indulge YOUR SOUL

CHAPTER 9
THE *Happiness* COCKTAIL

"Ever since happiness heard your name it has been
running through the streets to find you."
– *Hafez*

Thinking positively is a wonderful thing. It's the first step toward achieving happiness. And I have no real qualms with striving for happiness (obviously) except for two misconceptions: 1) the notion that happiness has the same meaning for everyone and 2) the notion that happiness materializes simply by thinking happy thoughts. As someone who has been to hell and back, I'll tell you what I've learned: happiness is a journey, littered with epic meltdowns and mortifying mishaps that are inevitable as we're only human. Happiness is a very personal feeling, and it's nobody's right to declare what it means to you. And most importantly, happiness is impossible if you're not willing to chase it.

I have had my share of highs and lows. A few years back, I was *that girl*. After going through a traumatic break-up with my boyfriend of seven years and losing my grandmother (who I was extremely close to) within the same week, it really was a miracle that I wasn't institutionalized. Though the break-up was kind of mutual and expected, it still hit me like a ton of bricks. My relationship was not healthy, and although I loved my boyfriend, I did not love the way he made me feel, which was not good enough, not skinny enough, not pretty enough, not *enough*. So as much as I really couldn't fathom losing what had become a family member to me, I knew ending it was truly the only way to save any shred of self-esteem I might have had left (which really wasn't much, at all), and live a normal, healthy life.

Months of hiding out in my apartment after the breakup in wine-stained Hello Kitty pajamas and surrendering my will to do anything besides drink vodka for dinner and drunk-dial people to keep myself entertained, really took a toll on me. I honestly in my gut thought I'd never come out of it. I was miserable. Actually, miserable is an understatement. I'm surprised I functioned at all. I spent countless hours spent analyzing all of my past actions, convincing myself there was something I could have done differently to save my broken relationship, or make him love me more. Couple that with some gut-wrenching emails and texts sent in a haze of tears and Merlot, and desperate pleas to give it "one more try" – I was truly one hot mess.

Prior to this humiliating display of pathetic behavior, I had never really experienced a meltdown of this grandeur. Sure, I had periods of upset and drama, but there was always a high to pick me back up again. My ex and I would break up in a horrifying shit storm, get back together, and things were good again, until the next hurricane. I was comforted by the chaos, in a weird way. But now I was out there, on my own, treading water without a life preserver; without someone to come pick me up out of the pool when the water got too deep. I had to figure out a way to climb out of it by myself. And above all, I had to figure out how to be happy.

The Champagne Glass is Half-Full

I launched my blog, "The Champagne Diaries", after deciding that I needed an outlet where I could be myself and express what I was going through. The blog's title was inspired by a good friend who encouraged me to choose champagne as my drink of choice as part of a new diet, as I mentioned in the introduction, but what came of it was so much more. I made the decision to be unabashedly, whole heartedly, Cara. And aside from being my true self, I made the decision to be happy. I quickly realized that the two went hand in hand.

Almost instantly, a fog felt like it had been lifted. I used my blog as a diary and documented all of the steps I was taking in my new life. I saw my break-up as an opportunity to find myself. I quickly learned what true optimism was, and began to view my champagne glass as "half-full." By definition, according to Mayo Clinic, "Optimism is the belief that good things will happen to you and that negative events are temporary setbacks to be overcome." This was the exact attitude I adopted, and it felt phenomenal.

The freedom to express myself was exhilarating, and soon enough, I felt like I had every reason in the world to celebrate myself and my life. I'd write posts about overcoming my dark times with inspirational, funny anecdotes. Women caught on. They related. They wanted to share their stories, too. Without realizing it, I had forged a community of effervescent, bubbly, hilarious women who wanted to motivate and empower each other. My readers became my support system, and somehow, in the midst of one of the scariest times of my life, I became theirs.

Happiness is a Choice, Anything Else is an Excuse

Ultimately, happiness is a choice, though sometimes it may seem like life has just handed us a bag full of lemons, dipped in shit. And even if you can recognize it's a choice, how do you turn that choice into action? To start, we need to accept that the hands we are dealt aren't always fair, but it's up to us to choose what we want to do with them. And you'd be surprised with just how much lemonade you can make from those shitty lemons.

Genetics do come into play when it comes to being a generally happy person; there is no doubt there. But don't be so quick to blame your depression on your mother or father. Scientific studies show that our personal choices account for 40-50% of our happiness. Do you realize how much power that gives you? Martha Washington once said, "The greater part of our happiness or misery depends on our disposition and not on our circumstances." And research on happiness consistently shows that the happiest people do not have better life circumstances than those who are unhappy. They just have a better attitude.

Realizing that you are in complete control
of your happiness is freedom. You can choose to
be optimistic, you can choose to shape your destiny,
and you can make the decision to look for the
good in every situation every day.

Realizing that you are in complete control of your happiness is freedom. You can choose to be optimistic, you can choose to shape your destiny, and you can make the decision to look for the good in every situation every day. Mastering this skill is not for the faint of heart, as it takes a lot of practice and blind faith, but once you achieve it, the reward is greater than you could ever imagine.

Let's take for example, my bubbly little blog. I would have never started "The Champagne Diaries" if my relationship hadn't fallen apart. I would never have decided to pursue my dream of writing this book if it weren't for the success of my blog. I would never have cultivated my creativity the way I did. I would never have learned to be comfortable in my own skin, and I would never have met the man who compliments me perfectly. I took my lemons and made a lemon drop cocktail (have you ever had one of those? If not, put this book down and go try one, now!). I chose the good life. I chose happiness.

If we can savor the moments where
things feel good, then the uncertain moments
are easier to pass through.

Make no mistake – the road to happiness is not completely paved with glitter. In fact, things can get a little messy as you're working toward being in a place where you can truly feel happy more often than not. But the key is holding onto the wins, the moments of success where you feel content. If we can savor the moments where things feel good, then the uncertain moments are easier to pass through (like for example, drunk dialing your ex-boyfriend and leaving him a voicemail of you singing a karaoke version of Cher's "If I Could Turn Back Time." Not that I've done that).

Your Happiness is Personal. Own it.

Another awesome thing about happiness? It's completely relative. If I ask someone what makes them fulfilled, and they tell me it's a brand new car and a giant house in the Hamptons, I'm not going to judge them. It's their choice. If it makes them happy, who am I to tell them they're wrong?

The same goes for those who find happiness in rescuing pugs or starting a family. Happiness is a very personal choice and it's up to you to decide what makes you feel good. The beauty of happiness is that nobody should tell you what it's made up of. If you can rely solely on what makes your heart swell, then that's all you'll ever need.

My personal idea of happiness changes all the time. Sometimes, happiness is chatting with an old woman in the supermarket, listening to her go on and on about how much she adores her husband, and how they've been blissfully married for fifty years. My heart could explode as she's giving me her secrets to a happy marriage, and in that very moment, I am completely and utterly filled with joy.

Other times, my idea of happiness is marching into Bloomingdales and tearing up the Michael Kors section, coming home with an arm full of shopping bags. And there is absolutely nothing wrong with that. One could argue that the latter scenario involves material possessions and is less sacred, but to me, a new leather purse is pretty fucking sacred. Both situations are blissful experiences, and they are *my* experiences. And if I find happiness in both, then that's just fine.

CHAPTER 10
MATTERS OF THE *Heart*

"But the most exciting, challenging and significant
relationship of all is the one you have with yourself.
And if you can find someone to love the you *you*
love, well, that's just fabulous."
– *Sex and the City*

One of the most defining things about our lives, as women, is
our relationships. The way we love, the way we fight, and the way
we ultimately recover from a broken heart shapes our lives like
nothing else. And it's impossible to sparkle if our hearts aren't
intact.

I clued you in briefly in the previous chapters about my relationship experience, and in case you haven't caught on, it all
sort of sucked up until now. Years and years of painful heartache,
having my self-esteem smashed up and blended into an organic
shit smoothie, and crying into glass after glass of Chardonnay
definitely shook me a bit. I'd love nothing more than to be able
to talk to my twenty-one-year-old self, as she was embarking on
her first real relationship, and tell her just how special she is, and
that she shouldn't settle for a man who won't commit. I'd love to
find that same girl at twenty-five, after the fifth break-up and tell
her "Don't you get it yet? This isn't working!" And I'd love to tell
that same girl at twenty-eight, as she was putting that long-term
relationship to bed one final time, that sometimes love just ain't
enough. But all of those things are what shaped me into the person I am today. And if had to have my heart fed into a blender a
few times, so be it. Those gut-wrenching experiences led to the
best parts of my life, and I wouldn't change a thing.

Enough is Enough

We've all been there: the girl who is waiting for him to change. Waiting for him to say he loves us, that he wants to be with us, that it only happened once. Waiting for him to finally introduce us to his mother or bring us around his friends. We make excuses, tell ourselves that he's just not ready yet; he's still getting over an ex who treated him so badly so we *must* be understanding. Of course, we must! We're the girl that's going to save his life! We're going to make him all better, make him emotionally capable of loving us like a normal, sane person would.

I once chased a guy for many years, convinced that I could Houdini him into a committed relationship. I was on a stealth mission to make him mine. Even after the four years it took to finally get him to call me his girlfriend, even after the cheating, the disappearing acts, and the total disregard for my feelings, I kept at it. And you know what? Eventually, I got him. And he was so uncomfortable being "that guy" that all we did was fight. He didn't want to be there, but he did it anyway, and he resented me for it – big time. The entire situation was completely unhealthy for both of us. We both tried to be someone else to make the other person happy, and in the end, we both wound up completely and utterly miserable.

Love should not be this bone-crushing,
complicated, painful experience.

If you currently fit into this category, follow these instructions immediately: turn off the Adele album, log off his Facebook page, and get it together, sister. What are you doing? Do you honestly think he's going to miraculously turn into the emotionally available man that you deserve? Ladies, hear me out: *you will never change a man.*

Sadly, most of us spend years chasing this impossible dream. And whether it's happening to us or our best friend, there is no "right" time to dictate when someone should get out of a relationship. I can't tell you when it's time to let it go; only you know that for sure. My mother once said to me, "When you've had enough, you will know." I repeated this to myself through every fight, every breakdown, until one day it clicked. I just didn't have it in me physically or emotionally to keep up with the charade.

I'll never forget the first conversation I ever had with my therapist after my break-up. In between the sniffles, I told the story of my relationship aloud, from start to finish. In short, I told the tale of two people who were desperately trying to make something work that was never meant to be. And they were ripping each other to shreds in the process. It all started to make sense to me. What the hell was I doing? Did I truly think this was the kind of love I was worthy of? Apparently, I did. And until I saw things differently, I forged ahead down a road of self-destruction that took years – and many ~~glasses~~ bottles of champagne – to clean up.

Love should not be this bone-crushing, complicated, painful experience. Sure, relationships have their ups and downs, but if you're forcing someone to be something they're not it's never going to work. And if someone is hurting you, disrespecting you, and making you feel like you aren't good enough for them, it's time to hit the road. Love should feel good. You should both be able to be yourselves, and it should work. At the end of the day, if you're trying to fit a square peg into a round hole, it's just not meant to be.

Be Better, Not Bitter

Once you're able to let this person go, the real work begins. It's so easy to get caught up in the details of what went wrong, who did what, and who was ultimately responsible for the demise of something you both probably thought would last forever. When a relationship ends, your heart is still on fire. It's impossible to be rational or level-headed when you've gone through such a whirlwind of emotions. You're still busy drafting emails or calling him repeatedly and hanging up to think coherently.

But eventually, the dust begins to settle and your tears begin to dry, and before you know it, you are able to slowly see the whole picture. You start to realize the part you played in the relationship, just as much as the part he played – for better or for worse. It's easy to get into the "what could I have done better" conversation in your head, and analyze every action you took, every word you said, but you just can't go there. You have to take comfort in the fact that you did the best you could. And through all the heartaches and all the mishaps, maybe he did, too.

You have to take comfort in the fact that you
did the best you could. And through all the heartaches and all the mishaps, maybe he did, too.

As ugly as it can be, you can't move forward if you're bitter. You have a choice: to live in misery, forever resentful of the person who broke your heart, or you can find a way to make sense of it all. Most of the time, it all boils down to the fact that you were just two very different people who wanted very different things.

And after a break-up, all you can hope is that you both finally become the people you were always meant to be.

Write Your Own Happy Ending

If someone had told me when I was going through my hardest times that all of it would lead me to the place I'm in today, I would have told you that you were out of your damn mind. I was so entrenched in a place of chaos and uncertainty that I never thought I'd claw my way out of it. And as bad as it was, the thought of starting over somehow seemed worse. Some people say that the point of certain relationships is to tear you down so that you have no choice but to build yourself back up. Well, let me tell you, I must have built the fucking Taj Mahal, because this took work.

The only way to come out alive after a bad break-up is to use it as an opportunity to get to know yourself again. It's so easy to lose yourself when you're so wrapped up in someone else. I could have told you every single detail of my ex's day right down to what he usually ate for lunch on Tuesdays, but if you had asked me what my favorite color was, all you'd get would be a blank stare. You become so focused on the "relationship you" that you start to forget the things that you enjoy. As tumultuous as it may seem, this precious time alone is the time to treasure. This is the time where you are raw, when it's all being hung out to dry. You get to learn from the past, and figure out what you want the next time around. This is the time you get to rewrite the rule book for your life.

I never expected to meet my husband and fall in love the way I did. Our first date lasted eight hours, and it only ended because the bar we wound up in closed for the night. We were *enamored* with each other. I remember one very specific thing about that date and it is this: I was completely and totally myself. I didn't put on an act or try to be something I wasn't. I was just me. And my husband loved every bit of it. And the best part? I felt the exact same way about him. We just made sense together.

My marriage is a love like I've never known. We respect each other, we're kind to each other, and we are a team. Things never get ugly. Even our bad days are never *that* bad. My husband's priority is making me happy, and my priority is doing the same for him. I would not have found him – or myself – if it weren't for every other piece of my life lining up the way it did. I had to date guys who were wrong for me to be able to appreciate the one who was right. I had to get torn down so that I could build myself back up and get to know myself at the core in a way I never thought possible. I had to be alone without the crutch of someone else to take the sting away. I had to fall apart so that something amazing could come together.

You get to learn from the past, and
figure out what you want the next time around.
This is the time you get to rewrite the
rule book for your life.

So whatever you are going through, remember this: you deserve nothing but gold. You should be with a man who loves every single thing about you: your smile, your passions, your quirks, your bad moods, your insecurities and your heart. And you shouldn't settle for anyone that you don't feel the exact same way about. Love can be so wonderful when you finally open yourself to up to the real thing.

CHAPTER 11
GOT TO BE *Real*

"Striving for excellence motivates you; striving for
perfection is demoralizing."
– *Harriet Braiker*

Ever have a day where you literally just burst into tears out
of nowhere? A day where no matter how hard you try to smile,
everything sucks? A day where you'd love nothing more than to
just crawl under the covers with a giant box of chocolate frosted
donuts and sulk? I've had more than I can count. And you know
what? It's not just okay, it's necessary. Let me explain.

Like I mentioned in chapter four, us girls just love to take on
the world. We have a tendency to try to do it all, and though we
always pull it off (duh!), we're usually fried by the time we're done.

One of the most exhilarating, inspiring, and completely exhausting periods of my life was when I was going to school to become a life coach. I was working my full-time job, taking classes
at night, practicing my coaching skills with classmates, being a
wife, and trying to remember to do minor things – you know,
like breathe, shower, and keep up with *The Real Housewives of
New Jersey*. My classes were demanding and I could barely keep
my head above water. I started wondering if I had made the right
choice. What if I was in too deep? I was terrified that I wasn't
going to be able to finish. And even if I finished, what if this
wasn't the right move for me? The self-doubt swept over me like
a tidal wave as I tried with every ounce of my being to pretend
that everything was alright.

I was also trying to juggle the blog and keep it light and up-
beat, when in reality I felt like an angry, worn-out troll on a daily

basis. How was I going to write about feeling glamorous when the bags under my eyes made me look like a raccoon? Who was I to motivate other women to be positive and cheerful when I felt like I was ready to bite someone's head off? I struggled deeply with this imbalance and my guilt began to pile up and eat me alive. I was losing my luster and I felt like the whole world could see it. I felt like a fraud.

It wasn't until I heard a podcast about embracing our emotions that I really got a handle on things. The psychologist talked about owning how you feel at all times. If you're pissed off, own it. If you're happy, own it. If you're confused as hell, own it. Go with the waves. Don't fight the bad days. Embrace it all.

Suddenly I felt a sense of relief. I had to accept the fact that I was not superwoman; in fact, I was a really stressed out woman who was taking on entirely too much. And I was allowed to have a breakdown. Nobody is perfect, and even if they were, who would want to be around them? We want to endure our struggles together. I know I don't want someone preaching to me who has never gone through a bad day. I want to hear it from someone who's been there, and has figured out a way to cope. I want encouragement from a survivor.

Breakdown Boulevard

Imagine coasting through life, never having to deal with any problems? It might sound great in theory, but think about how flat you'd be as a person. Lessons wouldn't be learned. You'd never see the full picture. You'd have no character. And you definitely wouldn't be able to appreciate the highs without the lows (and then what would we toast to?).

I've found that my greatest awakenings have come after hitting rock bottom. Take for example my journey into good health. I spent years drinking soda, gorging on lunches that consisted of white rice slathered in soy sauce, and dining on pizza for dinner at least three nights a week. I was a junk food queen. When I reached my lowest point, unhealthy, out of control, and sick of not being able to zip up my jeans, I knew I had to make a change. I had lost complete and total regard for myself and my body. I was in full breakdown mode, and something had to give.

I want to hear it from someone who's
been there, and has figured out a way to cope.
I want encouragement from a survivor.

When I adopted a new approach to healthy living, and really understood that the two went hand in hand, my breakdown turned into a breakthrough. I started to pick all the pieces up off the floor, and slowly put the puzzle together for the first time ever. My bad eating habits were a direct correlation to the value I gave to myself. I had to love and appreciate myself and my body before I could begin to treat it well. I lifted the veil that had blinded me for so long, and I emerged smarter, stronger, and on the road to a much better life.

You're Not Superwoman, so Take off the Cape

We've all heard the term "Superwoman" as being used to describe a woman who tries to accomplish everything at once. Marjorie Hansen Shaevitz wrote the book, "The Superwoman Syndrome," in 1984 which chronicled the characteristics of the overachieving woman who aims for a level of perfection that is just not attainable.

There's a reason that book was a best-seller. Most of us aim to be a superwoman in every area of our lives: at home, at work, with our friends and our family, at our volunteer jobs and with our hobbies and passions. In fact, I used to take it as a compliment when someone called me superwoman, until I realized it was burning me the hell out.

Superwomen suffer physically and emotionally. The stress of striving for perfection (which is a word that I want you to erase from your vocabulary immediately), can wreak havoc on us. Have you felt yourself going down this road? Women who fall into this category usually suffer from muscle aches, stomach cramps, irritability, mood swings, nervous ticks or twitches and insomnia. And that's just the tip of the iceberg, ladies.

Who decided it was healthy to work our asses off to the point of insanity? When did this become the ideal? Well, here's a brief history lesson: the Superwomen Syndrome was a product of the second-wave feminist movement in the 1960s. The first-wave of this movement was to gain legal rights and the second-wave involved sexuality, family, work, and reproductive rights. We wanted it all, and we got it all. And somewhere along we felt like we had to do it all – at once.

According to Wikipedia, today, more women earn bachelor's degrees than men, half of the Ivy League presidents are women and the numbers of women in government and traditionally male-dominated fields have dramatically increased. All of that is wonderful news for women, but how do we manage so much success and still maintain some level of down-time? Accomplishments are one thing; pushing to the point of excess is another. And, don't get me wrong; I am a huge supporter of women achieving all of their goals. I am all about doing your thing as long as you can do it with peace of mind and still make time for yourself.

There is one person in this world you
need to impress, and that is you.

So what possesses us to take on nine hundred tasks at one time? Believe it or not, many of us aim to achieve a superwoman status because deep down, we're insecure. We're looking for approval and we want to be perfect at everything. We feel like the more we do, the stronger we'll look. And if we juggle nine hundred balls without dropping a single one, we'll impress the world. But guess what? There is one person in this world you need to impress, and that is you. Think about the freedom associated with that. Imagine only having to answer to yourself? Not your mother, not your husband, not your sister or your best friend – just yourself. Surrendering that power to another person is a guaranteed way to lose your fucking mind.

Keep Calm and Cut Yourself Some Slack

I don't know about you, but I am really hard on myself when I get in a funk. As soon as my bad mood sets in, I enter panic mode. I know I'm going to be mad at the world for a good portion of the day, and I know there's not a damn thing I can do about it. The anxiety mounts and before you know it, I am a ball of negative emotions.

I can't stress how important it is that we cut ourselves some slack. Bad moods are going to happen regardless of how happy we are in general. You can feel great 90% of the time, but soon enough, the shit is going to hit the fan. Life's stressors can creep up on us at anytime, and things are not always in our control. And, let's face it; there are just certain times of the month when you're not in the mood for it. We have to allow for those days and realize that we're human and we need to give ourselves a little compassion when we're down in the dumps. In fact, that's the time when that self-compassion counts most.

And a new wave of research around self-compassion shows that being kind to ourselves will not just make our day better, it'll make us healthier as well. People who score highest on self-compassion tests are less depressed, have less anxiety, and are happier and more optimistic. And certain data around these studies also suggests that people who have self-compassion eat less and lose more weight. Do you really need to be convinced any further that being kind to yourself is the way to go?

So many of us are scared to show self-compassion because we fear we'll lose control (oh, how we love the control!) So many of us keep ourselves in check by negative self-talk, but we've gotta give it up, ladies. That behavior just ends us making us feel worse and takes a serious toll on our self-esteem.

And at the end of the day, all we can do
is our best. And that's more than enough.

Self-compassion is especially important when it comes to our eating habits. I have made a conscious effort to stop beating myself up when I eat something that I know isn't the healthiest for me. I used to fall into the trap of eating junk, feeling guilty over it, telling myself that I was never going to lose weight, and that I was a horrible person for eating that way. This, of course, led to me eating even more because I felt like a failure already. What's one more cookie? I had already devoured two, and those jeans are never going to fit anyway. Who can relate to *that* vicious little cycle?

Now, instead of the negative self-talk, I just move on. I'm kind to myself. I allow for the mistakes. I remind myself that I'm not perfect, and I never will be. Not every single thing I put on my plate is going to be perfect either. And, know what I've noticed? I wind up making much better food choices now. When I restricted myself from everything and told myself I was disgusting for wanting a slice of pizza, I'd usually wind up eating two. Now that I tell myself it's okay to indulge in something, I wind up having less of it. It's no longer emotional.

And the research is there to back me up. In 2007, researchers at Wake Forest University conducted a study where they asked eighty-four female college students to take part in what they thought was a food-tasting experiment. The women were all asked to eat doughnuts and candies. One group, however, was told by the instructor not to feel badly about eating the food and asked the women to not be hard on themselves. The other group didn't receive this message. And guess who ate more? The group of women who were given the mini lesson in self-compassion ate significantly less than the other group. Lesson learned: when you give yourself permission to eat, you don't over indulge.

So let's start being good to ourselves. We're human. We're going to mess up. We're going to cry. We're going to yell, and we're going to eat pizza. Hell, we're even going to eat doughnuts. And at the end of the day, all we can do is our best. And that's more than enough.

CHAPTER 12
THE POWER OF *Fabulous* THINKING

"You need to learn how to select your thoughts just
the same way you select your clothes every day. This
is a power you can cultivate. If you want to control
things in your life so bad, work on the mind. That's
the only thing you should be trying to control."
– *Elizabeth Gilbert, Eat Pray Love*

After my very first date with my husband, I immediately
called all of my girlfriends over. I sat them all down, and told
them I was going to marry him (now, before you write me off
as a total psychopath, please know this was an *amazing* first
date. Like the kind of first date you see in the movies: fireworks,
sparks, the whole nine yards. And he felt it, too, so I'm not that
nuts). Anyway, I sat my friends down, poured everyone a glass
of wine, and began gushing over my new man. I described our
whirlwind relationship to-be, our future wedding, and our life
together. *I just felt it.* I knew it was right. I wanted it. And I could
see it all laid out in front of me.

I am obsessed with visualization. After my first interview at
MTV, I envisioned myself working there. I pictured all of my
outfits, what my desk would look like, and where I'd go for lunch.
I saw myself walking through the lobby each morning, Starbucks
in hand, ready to take on the day. I even envisioned the phone
call from H.R. telling me I had gotten the job – right down to
the details of the conversation – and you know what? All of it
happened.

These may sound like little day dreams, but there is something to be said about visualization and thinking fabulously. Not

only did I land my husband and my job, but I had a positive outlook on both situations which in turn made me more optimistic. I confidently focused my energy on the things I wanted, and I got them.

Expecting nothing less than the most
fabulous result will set you up for success.

Sending out positive energy is crucial, specifically around situations where you are looking for a favorable outcome. Expecting nothing less than the most fabulous result will set you up for success. Even if you think there's not a chance in hell something might work out, you have to tell yourself it will. No matter what your current circumstances, expect nothing less than the best. You may have heard of *The Power of Positive Thinking*, but because this book is called *Sparkle*, we're going to give it an edge. We're going to call it: *The Power of Fabulous Thinking*.

Seeing is Believing

If you have trouble believing that visualization works, then get a load of this: brain studies reveal that thoughts produce the same mental instructions as actions. By creating visual imagery in your mind, the cognitive processes of the brain including perception, planning and memory are aroused. Your brain becomes primed for whatever it is you are imagining and it prepares for that exact outcome. Visualization has also been shown to increase motivation, self-confidence and prep the brain for success. The proof is in the pudding, girls. Now it's time to get creative.

So where do you begin? Well, first and foremost, you must apply the rule from the previous chapter that everything is possible. *The Power of Fabulous Thinking* does not work if you have already set limitations for your success. You have to truly believe that you can have whatever life you want. You can achieve any goal you set for yourself, and no dream is too big. You have the power to design the life you were meant to live.

Next, you need to close your eyes and picture a very specific goal. Be as clear as possible about this goal, so clear that you can imagine it happening right this moment, and all of the details are in front of you. You should imagine where you are, what you're wearing, who is around you, what the air smells like, what sounds are in the background, and most importantly, how you're feeling. Honing in on that exact feeling that you will have when you achieve this goal is key because it lets your brain connect to that emotion.

Maybe I'm feeling down or uninspired, but the
minute I exercise *The Power of Fabulous Thinking* I'm
propelled into a world that is sparkly, glittering,
and full of possibilities.

Repeat your visualizations as often as you like. I like to do them when I wake up in the morning as a way to jump start my day, or when I need a boost of motivation. Maybe I'm feeling down or uninspired, but the minute I exercise *The Power of Fabulous Thinking* I'm propelled into a world that is sparkly, glittering, and full of possibilities.

Aside from visualizing your success, write it down, too. Get a diary and take that same, specific goal and begin writing down exactly what it is, as if you've already achieved it. For example: *I am a hugely successful author with five best-selling books under my belt. I regularly host speaking engagements and split my time between New York and London. I'm about to work on my next book, which will be made into a movie.*

Remember what I told you: no dream is too big. We're thinking fabulous here, ladies! You can have whatever you want; you just have to believe it. I encourage writing your goals as often as once per day, if time allows, and at the very least once per week. And you want to make sure that you stay on track and regularly revisit these goals as a way to check in with yourself and measure your progress. Don't be discouraged if your dreams don't come true immediately; this isn't magic. But it's a guaranteed way to get a head start on your success and remain positive, hopeful and optimistic as you're working towards it.

Think Fabulous, Feel Fabulous

Here comes the fun part. *The Power of Fabulous Thinking* is just as much about setting and visualizing our goals as it is about believing we are fabulous on a day to day basis. When is the last time you actually strutted down the street? I mean really strutted, RuPaul style. You know that walk, the "I am woman, hear me roar!" strut. The kind of walk that makes a drag queen jealous. The kind of walk that makes construction workers spit out their coffee. The kind of walk that only a truly fabulous bitch can pull off.

I want you to try an experiment the next time you walk down the street. The first rule is you have to kiss any insecurities goodbye and not be concerned with what you're wearing or whether or not your mascara is smudged or your hair is frizzy that day. This is all about the imagination. I want you to envision yourself as a Victoria's Secret model (I like to pretend I'm Adriana Lima) and really pretend you are her – sick body, perfectly bouncy hair, flawless makeup. You're Adriana Lima, and you are stomping down a runway in forty-seven inch platform heels and a hot pink satin thong. You may or may not have angel wing pasties on your boobs. And you look hot.

Stay with me…

So there you are, parading down that runway (or 28th street, or the 2nd floor of the mall – minor details), doing that cute wink all Victoria's Secret models do to a random person in the audience. You have to-die-for pouty lips, sparkling with glittery gloss that is bouncing off the flashbulbs surrounding you. You get to the end of the runway and you blow a kiss – well, you don't have to go that far in this exercise – but you get the point.

So go ahead and give this a whirl. Make sure you wear at least a small heel; flats don't work in this exercise. Take note of how you feel, and how people react to you. It's all about confidence. I can guarantee that an extra five or ten pounds means nothing if you actually hold your head up high and tell yourself that you are the fierce, fabulous woman you know you are.

But don't try this without music. Make sure you have your iPod handy, and make sure you fire up a playlist that will give you the beat you need to rock that sidewalk. Here are some good tunes to get you going. Feel free to go put them on right now:

Chaka Khan "I'm Every Woman"
Lady Gaga "Born This Way"
George Michael "Too Funky"
Pink "Raise Your Glass"
Madonna "Who's That Girl"

I should also caveat this by letting you know that you're total-ly allowed to have a glass of champagne before attempting this exercise. In fact, I encourage you to. Lord knows those models drink it for breakfast before their big runway debut. But make sure you only have one glass. There's a fine line between lightly buzzed and disaster drunk. We don't want you tripping on the sidewalk and knocking out a tooth, because that would defeat the whole purpose of this little game and you'd probably never forgive me (or you'd sue me and make me pay for your dental work).

Here's another one. You are set to give a big presentation at work. Anxiety central! I don't think I know anyone who actually enjoys giving presentations aside from theatre majors. You know those people who get their rocks off by projecting their voices and speaking in slight British accents. But we all have to do it at some point, and there's nothing more un-fabulous than tripping over your own words and sweating like a hog in front of a room full of people.

This time around, you're going to do this *Sparkle* style and use *The Power of Fabulous Thinking*. You're not a senior analyst at a research firm; you're Mariah Carey being interviewed on *Oprah*. You have an entourage of people who glued hundreds of fake eyelashes and hair extensions onto your head that morning and assistants are waiting for you with bottles of Veuve Clicquot after you exit the stage. You are going to rock this presentation and you're going to rock it hard.

Give it a whirl and see how it makes you feel. I guarantee you'll be turning more heads and commanding more attention than you could have ever imagined. After all, would they expect anything less from a Champagne Girl?

CHAPTER 13
BE *Fearless*

"Above all, be the heroine of your life,
not the victim."
– *Nora Ephron*

I have carried a sense of fearlessness throughout my whole life when it comes to achieving goals. Sadly, this fearlessness does not translate into things like skydiving, but hey – you can't have it all. But I am fearless when it comes to going after what I want. I'm not scared of rejection, in fact, I welcome it. I don't make excuses. I take the leap all the time. To me, it's better to have tried something (and even failed miserably) than looked back on it later wishing I did. To me, I am responsible for making my life extraordinary.

Think about the last time you actually regretted trying something. Does anything come to mind immediately? Is there something you went after that may or may not have worked out, and you're kicking yourself for even trying?

Now think about all of the things you *never even attempted*. That stings a little more, huh? Most of us don't feel badly about trying things, or even sucking at them. But we all have regrets about the things we were too scared to ever take a chance on. And who wants to get to the end of their life and have a list of things they never got to do?

Australian nurse Bonnie Ware spent several years working in palliative care, caring for patients in the last twelve weeks of their lives. She interviewed her patients about the biggest regrets of their lives, and do you know what the number one regret was? Her patients confessed, "I wish I'd had the courage to live a life true to myself, not the life others expected of me." I'm not telling you this to break your heart (because honestly, how sad is that?) I'm telling you this so that you can save your own life.

What's Stopping You?

Let's start from square one. The question of the hour. The thing you must ask yourself when you are not moving forward: what the hell is stopping you? What's in your way? If you truly take the time to answer that question, you might surprise yourself when you realize that you can't come up with a valid answer – or at least one that I'll accept!

For the most part, when I ask anyone that question, they tell me they're afraid to fail. They're scared that they're not going to be able to pull it off. And that's a completely rational fear. We want to succeed. We want to be good at everything. But the real problem occurs when fear stops us from ever starting.

Nothing makes me sadder than seeing a woman who has so much talent but is too afraid to do anything with it. I am sure that there's something you've been dying to do but fear is holding you back. If that's the case, I want you to consider this: are you comfortable living a relatively content life, coasting on through and doing what's expected of you? Singing the same song everyone around you is singing? Or do you want to do something big, leave your mark on this world, and feel like you've contributed something new and exciting to those around you? Do you want to be extraordinary?

Of course you do! Who wants to just exist? I know you've got something you're just bursting at the seams over. We all do. And this is the time to get the hell over your fear and go for it. The first step toward growing a set of balls is taking action. No matter how small the step is, take it. Move forward with something. Sign up for a class, buy a website domain, or even just tell a friend your idea. Sometimes just putting it out there into The Universe is a great way to get started and have someone to hold you accountable.

Rejection is Your B.F.F.

Okay, so let's say you can get past the barriers and take risks to reach your goals – what do you do with the inevitable rejection that is headed your way? Let's be honest, it's not all going to be sunshine and champagne. Achieving success always comes with a few hiccups. You are more than likely going to mess up or encounter some issues, and there will most likely be some tears. I can guarantee you're going to want to throw in the towel at some point. But if you can learn to view those bumps in the road as blessings, you will be golden.

There is a quote by Oprah Winfrey that I have been known to tape to my computer screen from time to time. The fabulous Miss O once said: "The only people who never tumble are those who never mount the high wire." I remind myself of this quote often; through every setback, every "no" I hear, and every idea or plan that doesn't work out as I had hoped.

I started writing this book five years ago. When I wrote the first manuscript, it was a memoir. 50,000 words of a story I wanted to tell. Some of it was funny, some of it was serious, and some of it was just plain horrible. There was so much left for me to learn about myself, about writing, and about publishing a book. For one, I learned that I shouldn't have tried to publish a memoir at that point in my life. And not because I was twenty-seven – I had a story that I wanted to share and I believe it was a good one – but I didn't have the audience that would want to read it. And I didn't realize that memoir had the potential to turn into something even better. But I pressed on with that first book, hired a literary agent, and pitched it to major publishers. I had no idea what the process of pitching a book was like; I assumed that because my agent thought it was great, everyone would think it was great. I had no idea that the percentages of book deals that go to first-time authors are minimal, and that it's even bleaker for a first-time memoirist who has absolutely no fan base.

Fearless, I moved forward. The rejection letters rolled in. My agent forwarded some, others she told me about over the phone (I'm assuming those were the really brutal ones). Most writers would have fallen apart at this point. Writing a book and trying to get a book deal is one of the most gut-wrenching experiences of your life. The amount of time, heart and energy that goes into the entire process is enough to leave you flat-on-your-back exhausted, but dealing with the rejections from publishing houses you've dreamed of signing with is even worse.

But through each letter and each response from each editor, I made notes. I figured out what wasn't working with the book. The reasons were all the same: they really liked my story, but I had no audience. In publishing, the author is expected to have their own fan base before they get a book deal. I was so grateful for the rejection because it made me realize exactly what I needed to do to be able to launch a successful book. The "no's" made me better, and got me to a place where I could write an even better book and most importantly, have a kick-ass group of women who actually wanted to read it.

With Failure Comes Opportunity

Another beautiful thing about fearlessly failing is that you have a chance to do it all over again, and do it better. When my first book was rejected, I focused on the blog instead. I knew I wanted to grow my readership, but I had no idea that my book would take an entirely different shape than I first imagined. Soon after launching my blog, I began connecting with my audience. We shared experiences, triumphs, and tragedies. I shared my own personal stories, but I wove in lessons to each one that would apply to everyone. I used humor to soften the blow of some really harsh topics. I came into my own.

Fast forward three years and I completely rewrote my book. Filled with useful feedback and fresh new ideas, I figured out what worked and what didn't, and I built a brand new book that I was excited about it. With the new manuscript, I sought literary representation once again. This time, I had five agents who wanted to sign me. I chose the agent that was best for me, and we tweaked the proposal until we felt it was as close to perfect as possible. I was so incredibly proud of how far I'd come, and this time, I was *sure* we'd land an amazing book deal.

The book went out on submission to a grand total of nineteen editors. And guess what? They all rejected it. This time around, the feedback was similar: they all loved the book, but they didn't feel they could sell it. The niche was too small. And you know what I thought? *They were wrong.* At this point, most people would have thrown in the towel. But I believed in myself and my work. I had gained thousands of blog readers who regularly emailed me to tell me how excited they were for the book to come out. I had received unsolicited worldwide press including coverage in *Glamour*, *Shape*, *Cosmopolitan* South Africa, and one of London's biggest newspapers, *The Daily Mail*. Women from around the globe wanted this book, and I wanted to give it to them.

My new mantra was: get knocked
down seven times; stand up eight.

I wasn't taking no for an answer. I believed in myself. My new mantra was: get knocked down seven times; stand up eight. I was standing up and putting this book out independently. I refused to give anyone the power to take my dream from me.

Publishing this book independently has been a labor of love, but an experience that I wouldn't change for the world. I've never worked so hard in my life, and I have learned so much along the way. I realized that this was the better choice all along for me. This was where I needed to be. If you really think about it, failure became my beautiful second chance.

Everything is Possible

Once you've morphed yourself into a fearless fox, it's pretty easy to realize that you can achieve whatever it is you set your mind to. You have to believe that everything is possible. There is no other way. Do you hear me girls? Everything is possible.

Wrapping your brain around that can be pretty overwhelming. Imagine just looking at a life that you admire and knowing you can have it too? Do you know how much power rests in that thought? I'm not bullshitting you or blowing smoke up your ass. You can have whatever you want. You may not be able to have it immediately, and it may not come wrapped up in a pretty pink bow, but if you're willing to do the work, it can be yours.

I never let a day go by without believing that I will have everything I want. My goals are tiered, and I know that each step I take puts me in a better place for the next step. I'm on a train that is slowly chugging along, moving to my everything. Even when I get down, or stuck, I just remind myself to keep it moving. It's up to me to do the work, and keep the faith, and know that I will get there eventually.

You have to know in your heart that you deserve the life you want to live. That aching inside of you for something bigger and better is there for a reason: to propel you, to drive you, and to get you to that place where all the good stuff awaits. If you're willing to believe a little, and sweat a little, everything is possible.

You can have whatever you want. You may
not be able to have it immediately, and it may not
come wrapped up in a pretty pink bow, but if you're
willing to do the work, it can be yours.

DIGESTIF
A TOAST TO *You!*

Now that we've dazzled, sipped, and sparkled our way through this book, I want to thank you for allowing me to guide you through this journey. And I want to thank you for being open enough and brave enough to dig down deep into your soul and ask yourself some very big questions. You may want to go fill up your glass for this part, we've got some toasting to do.

When you're back, raise your glass with me, and know this...

I hope that if there was something you were scared to do, you found the courage and the strength to try it. I hope that if there is something in your life that is holding you back from smiling, you will gracefully let it go. And I hope that you have learned to focus on the beautiful woman that you are and forget about keeping up with those around you. You are more than enough.

For the women who struggle with their body image, please know just how gorgeous you are. It doesn't matter what size jeans you wear, it doesn't matter what the scale says; all that matters is that you are treating your body with the very best care. You've got one chance to live a healthy life. Do everything you can to be good to yourself, but don't forget to live a little. Once you stop beating yourself up for being human, a love for yourself will blossom that you never thought possible.

For the women who are trying to do it all: take a breath. Slow down and enjoy the little things. Life is made up of so many beautiful moments you're missing out on. Unplug, recharge, and reboot. Pamper yourself. Indulge. Take time to relish in the silly things; life shouldn't be so serious. Fill up the tub and kick your feet up.

And for the women who are nursing broken hearts: know that it will be okay. Every relationship is a chance to peel back another layer you never knew you had. Learn from the ones who let you down. Forgive them. Be better, not bitter. Make space for someone who loves you exactly as you are. The love you deserve is bigger than you ever imagined.

I hope this book has helped you realize that your happiness is one of the most important gifts you can give yourself. If there are things you want, go get them. You deserve them all. If there is negativity in your life, kick it to the damn curb. Fulfill yourself. Dream and do. Don't be afraid to fail. See rejection as an opportunity to get better. Accept nothing but the best in your world. Vow to live your most effervescent, sparkling, champagne life.

Here's to you.
Cheers.

ACKNOWLEDGEMENTS

Mom, without you, I would never have had the confidence to turn this book into a reality. Thank you for always coming along on my wild rides. Thank you for always letting me dream. And thank you for always letting me be me. I owe you everything.

Ryan, I could not ask for a more supportive husband. Thank you for believing in me and loving this project as much as I do. You continue to make me feel like the smartest, prettiest, coolest girl in the world. I love you forever.

To my brother, Mike. Who would have thought a dollhouse-loving brat and a dinosaur-obsessed mini genius would grow up to be best friends? I'm so proud to call you my brother. Thank you for everything.

Thank you to my family for being as loving, supportive, and crazy as you are (especially the crazy part.) I wouldn't have it any other way.

To my dearest friends Sabrina, Tara and Jen. You've been through it all with me. Thank you for letting me know when I lost my sparkle, and riding the waves with me while I got it back. I love you all so much.

Liron, without you I would never have fallen in love with champagne – or myself – the way I did. You came into my life exactly when I needed you. I know we are oceans apart, but I still think of you all the time. Thank you for motivating me and showing me just how much there is worth toasting to.

Cara Loper, you are an angel. You started as my designer and became my dear friend. Thank you for obsessing with me, supporting me, keeping me sane, and turning my vision into a reality. I'm ready to take over the world when you are.

To the The Bookmark Shoppe. There aren't enough words to thank you for everything you've done for me. Thank you for supporting and believing in a Brooklyn girl with a big dream.

Cara Lockwood, I could not have asked for a more supportive editor. Thank you for helping me make this book "sparkle."

Dr. Fritz, you saved me. Thank you for helping me get myself and my life back.

To my "Champagne Sisters" Mel, Charlotte, and Kiron. Who knew four girls in four different parts of the world could become so close? You have taught me the true meaning of sisterhood and I am forever grateful to each one of you.

And finally, thank you to my deliciously dazzling, wildly effervescent, kick-ass group of Champagne Diet fans. Without all of you, this book would not be what it is. You have inspired me more than you will ever know.

Made in the USA
Lexington, KY
23 July 2019